WEDDING FLOWERS

WENDY THOMSON & JOANNE HORNSBY

WEDDING FLOWERS

PRC

This edition first published in 2001 by
PRC Publishing Ltd,
8–10 Blenheim Court, Brewery Road, London N7 9NY
A member of the Chrysalis Group plc

ISBN 1 85648 598 6

Printed and bound in China

Page 2: A buttonhole made with Gerbera-weirdo.

Page 3: Rose.

Right: Roses.

ACKNOWLEDGMENTS

The publisher wishes to thank Simon Clay for taking all the
photography in this book, with the exception of the photographs
on page 40, which were kindly supplied by Jo Hornsby.

CONTENTS

INTRODUCTION

your choice of
flowers will enhance
the uniqueness of
the day

YOUR WEDDING DAY is one of the most special days of your life, and planning your wedding is an exciting time. This is a time when all your hopes and dreams for your special day start to become reality. Whether you opt for a traditional wedding or a more informal occasion, your choice of flowers will enhance the uniqueness of your day. This is an inspirational book, presenting lots of lovely ideas of the many ways that flowers can be used to add color, romance, fragrance, and symbolism to your wedding celebrations. In this book we will look at the many different types of floral decoration and adornment available for today's bride. There are many different approaches to using flowers: formal, informal, traditional, modern, naturalistic, minimalist, and abundant. We will be looking at the extensive range of choice open to the bride for the new millennium.

Fresh flowers have been used for adornment, decoration, and as a statement of emotion for thousands of years, but over the last four decades, with greater scientific understanding and advancement, commercial cultivation has created a vast worldwide flower industry. Today, a bride getting married in the spring may carry a bouquet including lilies from Holland, long-stemmed roses from Colombia, orchids from Thailand, and gypsophila from Britain. Modern temperature control technology has made all this possible. Price is a consideration, however, and although many flowers are available all year round, those confined to their natural season will generally provide the best value. It must be borne in mind that forced flowers are often less robust than those that are in season.

This book examines and explains the reasons behind the choice of a particular bridal bouquet and the practicalities of setting a theme for the whole floral contribution towards the celebration. A bride has to consider her physical characteristics when choosing a bouquet. If, for instance, she is fortunate enough to be tall and slim and is wearing a slim-fitting dress, then it would be appropriate to carry a long, linear design of, perhaps, lilies, dill, and white roses. A round posy definitely would not go with this style. These sorts of decisions and choices need to be made early on in the planning of a wedding to ensure that the dress matches the bouquet that will be carried on that exciting but somewhat dreaded walk down the aisle.

The flowers a bride chooses for her wedding usually have romantic or sentimental connotations, which often have strong links with the symbolism and traditions of the past. In the sixteenth century, rosemary was a popular choice for brides because of its long-lasting freshness after cutting. To signify constant love, bridesmaids would give the groom sprigs of rosemary tied with ribbons. These were meant to be an insurance for marital happiness. Anne of Cleves wore rosemary in her wedding headdress, but it didn't guarantee her a long and happy marriage to Henry VIII. Centuries later, Queen Victoria began a tradition for royal brides by including sprigs of myrtle in her bouquet. She planted a stem in the royal garden and sprigs of myrtle have been picked from this same plant and used in successive royal bridal bouquets.

While the symbolic and legendary meanings of flowers dates back to Elizabethan times, it was really the Victorians who assigned simple messages to individual flowers. The Victorian age of strict protocol and conformity inhibited the outward expression of emotions, so men and women used the beauty and color of flowers to express wishes and thoughts they dared not speak. Flower language became so important that *"durch die Blume sprechen"* (lit: speaking through flowers—"Say it with flowers") became a Western proverb. Early this century it was the bridegroom who chose the bride's bouquet and gave it to his betrothed as a wedding gift to express his

love. Today's bride chooses her own flowers. Modern tradition has it that all the luck and symbolism embodied in the bridal bouquet are passed on to the girl fortunate to catch it when it is tossed to the crowd as the bride leaves the reception or wedding party.

Today the "classical" style, though still popular, is giving way to many novel and innovative ideas—even at the top of the social tree. For example, when Sarah Ferguson married the Duke of York in the summer of 1986, she started a craze when she had her bridesmaids carrying decorated hoops. They had rarely been seen at wedding celebrations until she introduced them. Along with royalty, the weddings of famous celebrities also have a substantial

influence on what brides may decide for their special day. If a huge Hollywood star is pictured in one of the glossy magazines carrying a bunch of tulips, it is guaranteed many future brides will want the same. Florists have to be aware of the current trends and endeavor to keep one step ahead in their field of expertise.

Preparations and the planning of the wedding flowers can begin six to eight months before the big day with a visit to the florist. Designing flowers for a wedding is always a test and a challenge to any florist's skill and creativity. Careful planning is the key to arranging successful wedding flowers and will help ensure that the celebrations are faced with confidence. Flowers play a significant role throughout the day in the form of the decorations and adornments of the bride and her attendants, the flowers at the ceremony, and the floral displays at the reception. It is, without question, the bride's day and the flowers that she and her attendants carry are the most important of all, being the focal point from which the rest of the floral decorations take their cue. Corsages and buttonhole flowers, which are the modern equivalents of favors worn by knights to indicate their allegiance to a lady, should reflect the leading lady's (bride's) choice.

Take the earliest opportunity to visit the place where the ceremony will take place to plan the floral arrangements, to check on pedestals and any other suitable containers available; if possible take your floral designer with you. If you are having a church wedding, be sure to obtain the permission of the vicar, priest, or rector to allow you to decorate the church as you wish. Some churches have particular preferences or customs, and at certain festivals in the church calendar flowers may not be permitted. Most churches have their own flower arrangers and it would be tactful to ask to relieve them of their duties for the day. Go through the ceremony step by step to visualize the areas where the flowers will have the most impact.

Over the past fifty or so years the use of foliage in the wedding floral presentation has increased dramatically, mainly due to the wide varieties becoming increasingly more available. In 1940, the options available were probably little more than ivy or asparagus, but a new-millennium bride has a vast choice, ranging from the tiny heart-shaped anthurium leaves, the multi-colored codiaeum, or the sword-shaped ferns of the nephrolepis. Leafed branches and sprays of foliage can make stunning solo performances or can dress the stage for any kind of wedding design. Colorful and textured foliages have all the beauty of flowers and are as versatile, whether arranged as a cascading bouquet of ivy and myrtle, or forming the backdrop to a bouquet of calla lillies. Whichever way the foliage is used, it is sure to create a pleasurable impression.

Foliages are increasingly competing with flowers in floral arrangements and in some cases are more expensive. It is now widely accepted that foliage is a natural partner to a collection of flowers and, used artistically, will greatly enhance any arrangement. Few designs, be they formal, natural, or modern, will look complete without·a collar of leaves or foliage to balance and emphasize the different colors and textures. It is always a challenge for a florist to create a display using only a mixture of foliages. In this book we will demonstrate just how stunning a display can look using the smallest amount of flowers with a large array of leaves. Wind-fresh foliage can create sensational wedding bouquets and definitely must not be overlooked when assessing the options for your "look."

Spring, summer, autumn, and winter—each has its own special pleasures and delights which we consider in

separate sections. However, as explained earlier, many flowers are now available all year round, so there is a huge variety of flowers and foliage that can be incorporated into the bridal flowers, many of them steeped in symbolism or relaying a special message. We hope this book will help to inspire a bride in her choice of flowers—theme, mood, colors—to create the wedding of her dreams.·

"Some flowers spoke with strong and powerful voices, which proclaimed in accents trumpet-tongued, 'I am beautiful, and I rule.' Others murmured in tones scarcely audible, but exquisitely soft and sweet, 'I am little, and I am beloved.'

George Sand (Armandine A.L. Dupin) 1804–76

BOUQUETS

WHEN CHOOSING the bride's bouquet consider the color of the bridesmaid's dresses to make sure they complement each other. It is advisable to avoid too heavy a bouquet or one that needs delicate handling. The bouquet should not become a distraction in itself on the day. Bear in mind that the bouquet, although important, is an accessory and should not upstage the overall look. To keep the bouquet looking its best, keep it away from extreme temperatures and ensure that the stems of hand-tieds are kept in fresh, cold water until the last possible moment.

1 HAND-TIED: Perfect for a simple, modern wedding. Usually a loose round shape composed of roses, peonies, or anemones, and tied simply with ribbon or raffia.

2 FORMAL POSY: Traditional brides carry these and their bridesmaids usually carry an identical but smaller version. A round, even shape, they usually feature a tightly packed selection of roses in mid-bloom.

3 SHOWER BOUQUET: The classic church wedding bridal bouquet—a wired posy flowing down to a slender trail of flowers. A wide selection of blooms can be used, frequently in toning shades of white and cream.

4 TEARDROP BOUQUET: For traditional brides, it is similar to the shower bouquet although shorter and wider.

5 FREESTYLE BOUQUET: Personal and individual, it can be anything from a loosely tied bouquet using wild country flowers to a simple bunch of the brides favorite flowers tied with a pretty ribbon.

Traditionally the men in the wedding party, including the groom, best man, both the fathers, and the ushers, wear a buttonhole on the left lapel. Apart from the popular choice of carnation or rose, a good idea is to use one of the main flowers from the bride's bouquet for the groom's buttonhole.

EQUIPMENT
AND TECHNIQUES

EQUIPMENT

TRADITIONAL

The traditional shower bouquet is probably the most popular style for brides who still favor the traditional wedding dress. The bouquet must complement the dress with its full flowing skirts, small waist, and full sleeves. Many brides regard this traditionally romantic image as being their ideal for a wedding.

WIRES (Picture 1)

Wire is needed for making buttonholes, corsages, head-dresses, etc., and is available in nearly a dozen gauges of thickness. The four most widely used gauges are:

20 gauge (0.90mm). Available as stub wires. Used for wiring heavy flowers such as heavy-headed lilies and foliage.

22 gauge (0.71mm). Available as stub wires. Used for wiring medium-strength flowers such as roses and peonies.

28 gauge (0.38mm). Available as stub wires. Used for wiring more delicate flowers such as violets.

30 gauge (0.32mm) Available as stub wires and silver reel wire. Used for wiring very delicate flowers such as lily-of-the-valley.

1

STEM TAPE (Picture 2)

Widely used tape for covering wire stems, the natural green color making a perfect camouflage. The tape is also available in white and should be stored in a cool place to avoid perishing.

PAPER TAPE (Picture 3)

This was used a lot in the past for covering wires. It is available in white and green, but has not been used widely following the introduction of guttacoll and parafilm. Its main disadvantage is that the color runs if it gets wet.

FLORISTS' TAPE (Picture 4)

Two thicknesses of florists' foam tape are available in green and white. It is used to secure florists' foam into baskets or plastic trays.

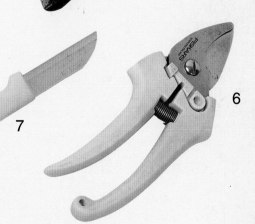

SCISSORS (Picture 5)

Florists' scissors are an essential specialist aid for all manner of tasks from trimming and cutting flowers and foliage to cutting ribbon. The scissors also have a customized notch for cutting wires.

SECATEURS (Picture 6)

Pruning shears essential for cutting the thicker stems of flowers and foliage.

KNIVES (Picture 7)

Specialist florists' knives for cleaning stems and cutting florists' wet foam.

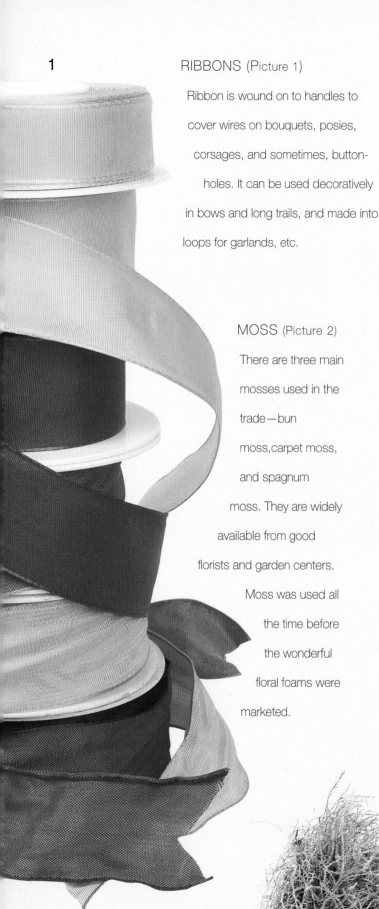

RIBBONS (Picture 1)

Ribbon is wound on to handles to cover wires on bouquets, posies, corsages, and sometimes, button-holes. It can be used decoratively in bows and long trails, and made into loops for garlands, etc.

MOSS (Picture 2)

There are three main mosses used in the trade—bun moss, carpet moss, and spagnum moss. They are widely available from good florists and garden centers. Moss was used all the time before the wonderful floral foams were marketed.

BALLS—POMANDERS

These are often carried by small bridesmaids. Ribbon runs through them to give something to hold onto, and they are available in wet or dry foams. They can be used for loose or compact designs.

PIN HOLDERS (Picture 3)

These are old-fashioned product and not used much anymore. They are heavy metal products available in all sorts of sizes. These, too, were used before we had floral foam.

HOOPS

(Picture 4)

Available in wood or plastic and all sorts of sizes ranging from six to twenty inches, these became hugely popular after the marriage of Sarah Ferguson to Prince Andrew, but are not so popular today.

MODERN

The hand-tied or "continental" bunch has become one of the most popular forms of bridal bouquet. The flowers and accompanying foliage are carefully arranged in the hand, and the stems are spiraled to create a three-dimensional design, usually in a linear form, for the bride to carry.

WIRE—THIN GOLD (BULLION) (Picture 1)

This thin gold wire is relatively new and is entwined around displays for decoration.

PARAFILM

The newest addition to the florists' tape family. This particular one has to be stretched when applying it to wires. Use this or gutta percha, whichever you prefer.

COMBS (Picture 2)

These are simply normal hair combs to which corsages of flowers are added.

ECO-BAND

Used for tying hand-tied designs.

ALICE BANDS

(Picture 3)
Ordinary hair-bands—plastic, wooden, or covered in material —to which flowers are either glued or wired.They are normally worn by bridesmaids rather than brides.They tend to look too heavy for the bride.

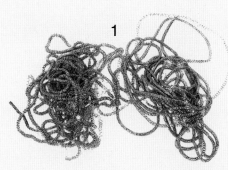

PEW END CAGES (Picture 1)

These are filled with wet floral foam and are designed to clip over the ends of pews in church. They are easy to use and saves you having to tape foam onto the pews.

BOUQUET HOLDERS (Picture 3)

Another revolution which saves so much time. Every bouquet had to be wired until these came along. Their main advantages are that they can be made up in advance and that in the summer you need not worry about watering the flowers.

MINI DECOS (Picture 2)

A very small dome of floral foam covered in a plastic cage. Ideal for making small designs for cakes or champagne bottles.

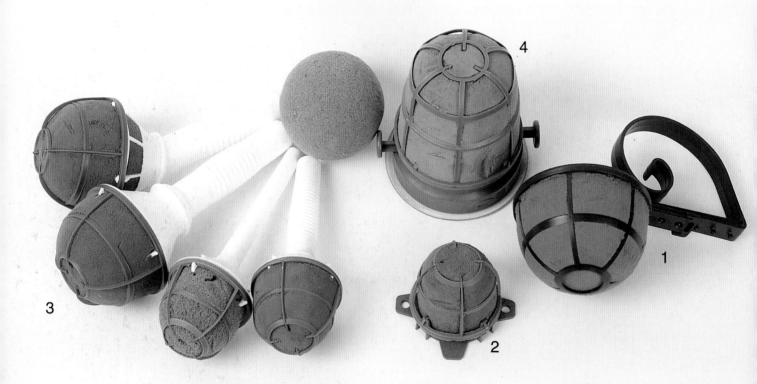

CAR-DECO (Picture 4)

A large dome of floral foam with a suction device on the base. This ideal accessory allows designs to be put onto the front of cars. The suctioned base sticks securely to bonnets without any damage or any unecessary fuss.

1

PAPER RIBBONS (Picture 1)

A relatively new idea to reach the commercial florists' market, this ribbon is beautiful when used for wedding work. It has to be unraveled though—very time consuming when in a hurry!

RAFFIA

Used as much by gardeners as it is by florists, especially in its natural color tone—the one that looks like straw. This ribbon/tie is wonderful when creating a very natural kind of wedding design. It is also being used much more now for everyday commercial use.

HESSIAN

Another rustic kind of ribbon, which up until a few years ago would never have been seen in a florist's shop! As everything is going back to being very natural and rural, this is a great ribbon to use for garden-style weddings, and works particularly well when used with flowers such as sunflowers and things such as wheat and barley.

SILK THREAD RIBBON (Picture 2)

A very new ribbon to the market and one that is not very waterproof—so take care when using it. Papery to the touch, it has very small silk threds running through it, and is available in a huge range of colors.

WILLOW BALL

A new and fun idea for weddings—a ball made from willow. You can either create something inside the ball (with a lot of patience!) or something can be made on the outside. This is a great one for those smaller bridesmaids.

TWISTED WILLOW

Also known as contorted willow, this wonderful twig is bought by the bunch—unless you are very lucky and have a contorted willow tree in your garden. This is wonderful when used in wedding work and gives a very modern yet natural look to the wedding being created.

2

TECHNIQUES

WIRING

A LEAF

Take a 0.26mm gauge wire and stitch through the leaf along the vein (doing all 3).

Take the remainder wires and wrap around the leaf stem.

Taking some form of ste
wires—pulling tape taut

A CARNATION

Taking a 0.71mm & 0.56mm wire.

Bend the end into a loop.

Holding the wire up to t
of the wire and wrap arc

A ROSE

Take a rose head with stem approximately 1 inch long and insert up the stem a wire of 0.71mm.

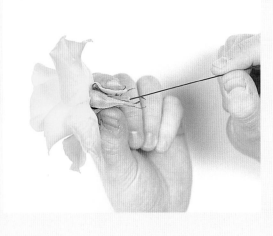

Using some stem tape, starting from the top, wrap around the wire from the base of the rose head. . .

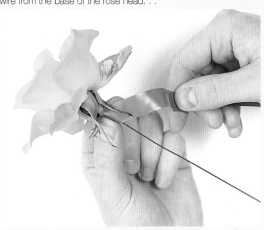

. . .all the way down.

ound the exposed

Tape all the way down to the end of the wire.

Try to achieve a neat finish.

ower, take the other end
secure.

Taking some form of stem tape, wrap around the
exposed wires, pulling tape taut.

Finished product.

Finished product.

DAISIES

DOUBLE LEG MOUNT METHOD
Using a 0.71mm wire bend in half and wrap one of the ends around the stems of your flowers.

This leaves you with two legs of wire

Making a bow

A BOW

Taking approximately one meter of ribbon (one used is polyproylene). Make a single loop, then make into a figure of eight.

Fold ribbon back over again leaving you with four loops and two tails.

Using a thinner piece o the middle and tie secu

pe as before with stem-wind

e of ribbon tie, scrunch

Repeat this method.

Join two together and finish.

SPRING WEDDINGS

SPRING IS TRADITIONALLY the perfect time for marriage with its symbolism of rebirth and new beginnings. The season heralds a mood of bold design and pared down simplicity. It is a season with a wonderful fresh look, and yet has a cool sophistication about it. Spring provides a mixture of crisp, bold colors and fresh, delicate flowers—from newly cut Dutch tulips to the most classical of British daffodils. The scents of spring complement the bright greens, yellows, and whites of the flowers and foliage. The great variety of flowers available combine to give a wealth of textural contrasts to any spring bouquet.

Sound of vernal showers
   On the twinkling grass,
Rain-awakened flowers,
   All that ever was
Joyous and clear, and fresh, thy music doth surpass.

From To A Skylark by Percy Bysshe Shelley (1792–1822)

Birthday Flowers in Spring

PISCES (FEBRUARY 19 – MARCH 20)

COLORS: Soft green, silvery white

White Lily (*Lilium*)

Daffodil (*Narcissus*)

White Zinnia (*Orchidaceae*)

ARIES (MARCH 21 – APRIL 19)

COLOR: Red

Safflower (*Carthamus*)

Red Carnation (*Dianthus*)

Muscari (*Grape hyacinth*)

Red Rose (*Rosa*)

TAURUS (APRIL 20 – MAY 20)

COLORS: Pink, pale blue, pale green,
emerald green

Mimosa (*Acacia*)

Poppy (*Papaver*)

Pink Rose (*Rosa*)

Lilac (*Syringa*)

MEANINGS OF SPRING FLOWERS

CARNATION, red—Unrequited love, "alas for my
poor heart"

DAFFODIL—Flower of March—Regard and Hope

HYACINTH—Game / sport

LILAC—First emotions of love

LILY, white—Purity*

MIMOSA—Secret love

POPPY—Consolation

ROSE, pink—Sweetness

ROSE, red—Love (from the earliest times the rose
has been associated with love)*

ZINNIA, white—Youth and old age

BRIDES

MODERN

This lovely hand-tied design (RIGHT) is ideal for the spring bride who wants a modern and unstructured design. The multitude of colors and the way the tulips are used create a stunning effect and help give the bride great choice. The design consists of "Crispa Creme" tulips entwined with the elegance and freshness of *Vibernum opulus* "Roseum" and is finished off with contorted willow.

beautifully soft, white ranunculus combined with softly scented dill (*Anethum*) and the hugely popular bupleurum. The design is completed with some variegated pittosporum to create a wonderful natural-looking arrangement.

NATURAL

A design for the bride who wants a "just picked from the garden" look. The stems of this hand-tied arrangement (BELOW) are designed to spiral and are supposed to be left

exposed. It is customary for these designs to be tied with a bow of natural looking material such as hessian or raffia. This arrangement consists of

TRADITIONAL

A couple of decades ago wired bouquets were all the rage, but the amount of work involved inevitably meant working this way cost more than anything designed in foam. Having said that, if you can afford a wired bouquet, the designs can be staggeringly beautiful.

This "shower" (RIGHT) is designed for the bride who lives and breathes tradition. The bouquet is arranged around freesias, tiny delicate flowers well known for their lovely scent. In this pretty design the freesias are incorporated with the larger lilies and roses to create a cascading wired bouquet. The design consists of "Blue Heaven" freesias, "Pistach" roses, "Benary Blauw" trachelium and stunning "Royal Fantasy" lilies. The finished arrangement is complemented with the naturalness of rose leaves.

BRIDESMAIDS

LEFT: A beautifully simple yet natural twig basket filled with tulips is ideal for little bridesmaids— rather than older ones—and is just perfect for the spring season. The design consists of "Crispa Creme" tulips with bottle-green reindeer moss, and is finished off with an appropriate yellow satin bow.

ABOVE RIGHT: A traditional design made on a foam holder, this is based on the old Victorian posy, which consists of consecutive rings of flowers. Any mixture or a single variety of flower can be used. This design is finished off with some white tulle to create a nice effect and to give the bouquet a beautiful outline—it would be the perfect complement if the bridesmaids had tulle on their dresses. The design consists of a "Pistach" rose which is then surrounded by sweet-scented "Blue Heaven" freesias. The next ring is of "Pistach" roses with the third ring consisting of the elegance of "Crispa Creme" tulips. The bouquet is then filled in with "Benary Blauw" trachelium.

BELOW: This pomander ball design is light to carry and is fun for the smaller bridesmaids. The design is constructed on a small ball of wet florists' foam and a ribbon handle of choice is attached to the ball by means of a wire. If the ends of the wire are hooked, the handles are perfectly secure so there should be no worries about accidents. This spring design has the contrast of bright and radiant "*Vymini Santini*" chrysanthemums and dyed green reindeer moss—they combine to create a lovely alternative from the norm.

BRIDESMAIDS' HEADDRESS

Bridesmaids' headdresses can really add an effective finishing touch to the overall wedding look. Made correctly, they are light and easy to wear. Young bridesmaids not only find them fun but headdresses make them feel very special. The size of the bridesmaid should be kept in mind—a good tip is to measure the heads of the girls who will be wearing them!

The wired half circlet shown here is designed to be worn toward the back of the head (this is where the measurements should be taken in this case). It consists of "Pistach" roses, pale purple "Blue moon" freesias and purple "Benary Blauw" trachelium with variegated pittosporum as the chosen foliage.

SPRING GUESTS

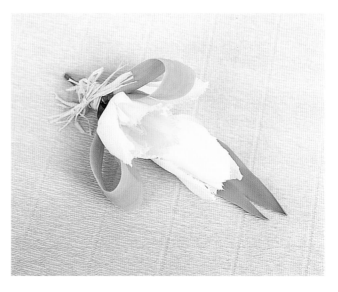

AS WELL AS YOUR personal flowers, it is pleasant for your guests to celebrate your special day with their own flowers. In the modern trade there is virtually no limit to a florist's creative art—almost any clothing or accessory can be decorated. They need to be, for today a wide range of outfits are worn to weddings and it is not so important to attend a wedding conservatively dressed. The men in the wedding party—the groom, best man, both fathers and ushers—usually wear a buttonhole, always on the left lapel. The most popular choice is the carnation but a more flamboyant alternative that goes with the general theme can be created.

For spring this is a delicate buttonhole (ABOVE RIGHT) made from "Crispa Creme" tulips using the flower's leaves and finished with a natural raffia bow.

The "Blue Suede Shoes" (BELOW) are for the more daring who want to be a bit different—and why not? Today's florists are very versatile and shoes can be decorated with almost any type of design. These blue shoes are a beautiful shade verging on the lilac. They are complemented with some dainty "Charm Picotee Blauw" lisianthus (*Eustoma*) which is surprisingly hardy considering its delicate appearance. In this case the flowers are wired and backed with subtle variegated ivy. The design is then wired onto the beautiful bluecolored shoes to create an elegant effect.

A decorated clutch bag (BELOW) can create a perfect accompaniment to a wedding outfit. This is ideal for the warmer months where a corsage may "pull" the material of the more flimsy outfits often worn at this time of year. Clutch bags are an excellent accessory as they serve a dual purpose. They afford the sheer delight of having some flowers for the special day, plus the very practical purpose of actually carrying things. The flowers are attached to the bag using a wire mount which does not damage or scar the bag in any way. The contents of this design are cream "Bossa Nova" freesias complemented by variegated ivy (*Hedera helix*).

RECEPTION

WHETHER THE RECEPTION is in a hotel ballroom, a restaurant, local hall, or even outdoors, some background work should be done to establish which kind of flowers are going to look best in the location. The floral decorations should have a strong link to the theme used in the rest of the wedding designs. With the expansion of the flower industry over the last ten years, there are many options open to today's bride and she has almost unlimited choice all year round.

In most cases the way a bride plans her floral decorations echoes her personality. There are no rules as to how daring or traditional a bride should be, and in this case we show something quite different. Tulips are traditional spring flowers but are seen as modern when used — as here — as the basis for a reception.

This garden-style design for the top table (ABOVE RIGHT) consists of cream "Crispa Creme" tulips and beautifully delicate muscari (grape hyacinths) combined with yellow forsythia. Pussy willow has been added for a natural look. A tray is filled with florists' foam and then covered in moss. The flowers are inserted into the foam giving the novel impression that they are growing naturally from the moss creating the wonderful effect of a spring garden.

A similar design (BELOW) employing the same plant materials is used for the other tables. Here, instead of a tray, a wire basket is filled with florists' foam and covered with carpet moss. It is essential to ensure that the basket is watertight. The basket is filled with the same flowers as above but, instead of being an elongated design, it is an all-round posy.

Designs for arrangements for the guests tables can, of course, be different from the top table, but it is generally more effective to "theme" the reception. A wide range of different designs can tend to look a little bitty and undecided.

WEDDING CAKE

The wedding cake is invariably the focal point of the reception repast. In some wedding planning, a really unusual wedding cake is commissioned; in other cases the cake is left to last and decorated at the last minute. Some of the more elaborate cakes can be made to look like floral masterpieces but can run the risk of being too over the top and ruining the general effect.

Springtime conjures up soft breezes, blooming bulbs, and fresh fragrances, and the design for this cake incorporates the soft, elegant, pastel shades ideal for the joys of the season. This decoration uses typical springtime flowers— lilac "Blue Heaven" freesia, "Million Stars" gypsophila and limonium (*Latifolium*). The design (ABOVE) is a wired circlet simply placed on the two-tiered cake.

THANK YOU

Traditionally the mums or important ladies in the wedding party—grandmothers, best friends, etc.—are given a fresh bouquet of flowers as a thank-you for all the help put into the wedding day. It is always a nice idea to show how much people are appreciated, and it makes them feel that extra bit special. It is usual for these to be presented during the speeches at the reception.

A simple spring bouquet is a standard, traditional design but makes a lovely gift. It is always a nice idea to use the same type of flowers in your wedding bouquet in the thank you gifts. This is an especially good idea for the bride's mother as it might remind her of her own wedding day.

The design (ABOVE) includes green peas (*Denranthema chrysanthemum*), "Casablanca" September flowers, "Royal Fantasy" cream lilies, "Charm Picotee Blaauw" cream lisianthus, "Kees Nelis" tulips, "Dianthus Solar" carnations, and yellow "Frisco" roses.

A beautiful basket arrangement (RIGHT), incorporating a bottle of champagne, is a little different and an agreeable option to the traditional bouquet. The basket arrangement is a good idea for weddings in the warmer months. The flowers are arranged in florists' foam, and will stay fresh looking even if they are left lying around for some time before the presentation as is often the case.

Included in this arrangement are "Bossa Nova" cream freesias, "Columbe de la Paix" calla lilies, cream "Pistach" roses, *Eucalyptus populus*, bear grass (*Xerophyllum tenax*), and variegated pittosporum.

SUMMER WEDDINGS

SUMMER BRINGS a splash of color and an abundance of richly perfumed blooms to celebrate the warm joys of the season. It is difficult not to want to be a summer bride when the florists are brimming over with a riot of colorful and scented flowers. The fields are abundant with arrays of wild flowers and foliage, and the rich fragrances float and linger in the air on the balmy, sunny days. Bring the season out of the garden and into your wedding! Summer flowers are soft and flowing with favorites such as lilies, roses, delphiniums, and scabious.

I know a bank whereon the wild thyme blows,
Where ox-lips and the nodding violet grows:
Quite over-canopied with lush woodbine,
With sweet musk-roses, and with eglantine.

From *A Midsummer Night's Dream* by William Shakespeare (1564–1616)

Birthday Flowers in Summer

GEMINI (MAY 21 – JUNE 20)

COLOR: Yellow

Lily of the Valley (*Convallaria*)

Sweet Pea (*Lathyrus*)

Lily (*Lilium*)

Tuberose (*Polianthes tuberosa*)

CANCER (JUNE 21 – JULY 22)

COLORS: Smokey gray, silvery blue,
iridescent blue

Lace flower (*Ammi*)

Iris

White Rose (*Rosa*)

Arum Lily (*Zantedeschia aethiopica*)

LEO (JULY 23 – AUGUST 22)

COLORS: Orange, golden yellow

Pot Marigold (*Calendula*)

Sunflower (*Helianthus*)

Peony (*Paeonia*)

Palm (*Cycas*) — cut foliage

MEANINGS OF SUMMER FLOWERS

ARUM LILY — Magnificent beauty

BLUEBELL — Constancy

HOLLYHOCK — Ambition

IRIS — Message of promise

LARKSPUR — Flower of July — Appreciation

LILY-OF-THE-VALLEY — Return of happiness

ROSE, white — Spiritual and true love (I am worthy of you)

SUNFLOWER — Splendid

SWEET PEA — Departure (once cut the Sweet Pea is
extremely short-lived)

TUBEROSE — Dangerous pleasures (its heady scent
can almost make you faint)

BRIDES

MODERN

What is a florist's definition of modern? It could be something way-out, something using unusual flowers and foliage, or simply something that you do not see brides carrying down the aisle every day. Actually, it could be any of these or a mixture of all three. The season normally evokes impressions of warm weather, holidays and of course beautiful summery weddings. Marketing departments are busy getting their mood boards assembled and brides are thinking about what they can have on their special day.

This design (ABOVE RIGHT) for a modern summer bouquet is both striking and unusual, suitable for a bride planning a very personal and individual day. This easy-to-carry, over-the-arm, design is very dramatic. It comprises double "Echo Geel" cream lisianthus and is perfect for the modern bride wanting a colorful wedding, as these beautiful flowers come in every shade from white through to purple. They create a stunning contrast with the absolutely gorgeous green "Shamrock" chrysanthemum which matches the elegant "Black Beauty" cream calla lilies (*Zantedeschia*). The bouquet is based with large butterfly aspidistra and palm leaves (*Cycas revoluta*) and finished off with a natural sacking bow.

TRADITIONAL

This summer bouquet (BELOW) stays well away from boring pinks and peaches and opts to go blue. The design would suit the bride having a traditional church wedding. Classic bridal bouquets such as this were brought back into fashion in Britain in the early 1980s when the late Princess Diana had one for her wedding day. Prior to this event they were generally seen as being old fashioned, but this is not the case any more.

The bouquet (BELOW LEFT) has been wired from start to finish, a very lengthy job that should really only be undertaken by a skilled florist. The design consists of striking "Blue Bee" delphiniums combined with the elegance of "Bianca" roses, double "Echo Geel" cream lisianthus, and white "Lake Powell" trachelium. The arrangement is entwined with delicate pittosporum foliage. All of these combine to create a cool yet stunning wedding bouquet.

NATURAL

A hand-held design is a loose, round-shaped design which can consist of any flower and foliage of choice. A half hand-tied design finished off with an elongated tail, which in this case has been wired. This design (RIGHT and ABOVE RIGHT) uses the amazingly beautiful "Stargazer" lilies,* highly fragrant flowers, which have become increasingly popular for weddings. The lilies are combined with "Bianca" roses and delicate "Million Stars" gypsophila, which helps to lighten the design. The arrangement is backed with deep green, soft ruscus then tied together with a simple white paper ribbon bow.

*If you suffer from hayfever, or can't stand strong-smelling flowers, then we would advise against this particular variety of lily.

BRIDESMAIDS

ANY GOOD FLORIST will help to inspire and enthuse you to create your wedding day dream, and an important facet of this is helping you find the perfect match for the bridesmaids' flowers.

Here are six different inspirations for the hot season! The first three are ideal for hot summer days because they have been designed on holders which contain florists' foam which has been soaked with water before flower application. This helps keep the flowers beautifully fresh and can keep them good for up to three or four days—perfect if you are thinking of having any of your wedding flowers preserved.

Pure white and simple creams (ABOVE) combine to help make this bridesmaid's bouquet simple yet elegant. Designed on a bent bridal holder, this is commonly known as a "posy." Included in this bouquet are the fashionable mini white "Siby" gerberas, white stocks (*Matthiola incana*), white dill, and double "Echo Geel" cream lisianthus, all topped off with variegated pittosporum.

A contemporary modern design (LEFT) consisting of "Stargazer" lilies combined with "Tineke" roses and white wax flower orchids (*Chamelaucium unicatum*). These flowers are arranged with an array of unusal foliage which include, bamboo grass, butterfly fern, cordyline leaves ("Rededge") and oval-leaved eucalyptus.

This design (RIGHT), constructed on a straight bridal holder, also has the modern approach. It is an upright, more European, design in tones of cool blues and summery creams. The bouquet consists of "Blue Bee" delphiniums, beautifully scented white sweet peas (*Lathyrus odoratus*), wild looking white dill, and double "Echo Geel" cream lisianthus, all with a background of scindapsus leaves (devil's ivy/golden pothos).

FAR RIGHT: This bouquet is really something quite different, yet simple and very elegant. It is a hand-tied design which depicts the image of a freshly picked bunch of flowers. This is ideal for a natural-style of wedding day and for anybody who hates sticking to the norm! It consists of "Million Stars" gypsophila and white "Bianca" roses and is finished off with the comparatively unusual dieffenbachia leaves.

RIGHT: These bridesmaids' bouquets are designed to match that of the small bridesmaid shown below. All are hand-tied designs and consist solely of the sophisticated white "Pompeii" lilies (which have an extremely strong perfume, so should be avoided by hayfever sufferers). The stark beauty of these flowers make quite a statement about a bride's personality. The lilies are mixed with the wild and wispy bear grass (*Xerophyllum tenax*) and variegated pittosporum. The arrangements are finished off with a white crepe bow.

A design (LEFT) known as a "Victorian Posy," this consists of five consecutive rings of flowers on a wet foam bridal holder. This particular one is finished off with white tulle matching the bridesmaids' dress.

The design consists of the poppy-like "Mona Lisa" blue anemones which bear a striking resemblence to the wild poppy. These are combined with double cream "Fuji Yellow" lisianthus and "Bianca" roses. Although there are five rings to this arrangement, only three different varieties of flowers have been used, but the plants have been used at different maturity levels. This all combines to give a beautiful alternative for a young "princess!"

GUESTS

THERE IS A variety of floral accouterments available for your guests on your special day, ranging from simple corsages to more intricate designs such as handbag or hat arrangements.

Shown here are four quite different ideas for the guests coming to your wedding.

This white hat decorated with "Stargazer" lily (RIGHT) is ideal for the person who loves wearing hats. The flower is carefully sewn on to the ribbon rim on the hat so as not to damage it.

A novel, pink, fluffy bag (LEFT) is a fun alternative to the traditional handbag. Items like this are becoming much more fashionable and are ideal for that someone who wants to look a bit different. The design is delicately sewn onto the bag and consists of a single white "Pompeii" lily, and "Charm Picotee Blauw" lisianthus to which small-leaved variegated pittosporum is added.

buttonholes are the most practical accessory on a wedding day, so are very popular. This corsage, complementing a banana yellow jacket, comprises "Blue Bee" delphiniums and double "Echo Geel" cream lisianthus. White "Lake Powell" trachelium is included to add color and, to create a natural look, the foliage from the trachelium is used.

N.B. most good florists will pin items like this for you, so that you do not have to scrabble around looking for a pin after the florist delivers to you.

ABOVE: Here is the ideal accompaniment to a lovely summer outfit. The majority of brides' mothers inevitably like to carry this sort of handbag design as it helps to make them feel that extra bit important. The design is attached to this beautifully decorated accessory by covered wires and will in no way hinder the practical use of the handbag on the day. This handbag is decorated with the dendrobium Singapore orchids—the largest genera of orchid, which is available in a considerable diversity of form. This particular variety is "Madame Pompadour Wit" and is combined with "Million Stars" gypsophila and ivy (*Hedera helix*).

RIGHT: Although simple, this corsage can look as classy as something more extravagant. Corsages and

RECEPTION

THESE CREATIONS for the summer season are a little different, using lemons and limes as the central idea

For the top table design a fish bowl vase is used (ABOVE RIGHT). The vase is filled with lemons and limes, mixed with green marbles, and placed on top of a dish filled with floral foam. Sliced lemons and limes are used as well whole ones, to allow the scent of the citrus fruits to fill the room. The actual design consists of strikingly bright "Blue Bee" delphiniums, double "Echo Geel" cream lisianthus, "Bianca" roses, dill (which looks suspiciously like cow parsley) and novelty pineapples (*Ananas*). These flowers mix well with the chosen foliage of variegated pittosporum, hard and soft ruscus, and bear grass (*Xerophyllum tenax*). The combined flowers and foliage, along with the zest of the fruit, just shout summer, and it makes for a very different display.

LEFT: The guest tables consist of exactly the same flowers, but they are arranged in a very thick, tall glass vase. This gives the arrangements some height but does not obstruct or inhibit the guests' social interaction.

To complete the overall effect it is a good idea to have the top table decorated with some foliage as it takes away the potential plainess of the "important" table and finishes the room off. Soft ruscus is carefully pinned to the cloth, which has been simply decorated with cream crepe paper bows (ABOVE) to create a beautiful and fresh effect which helps to make your day perfect. Any reputable florist will be able to make this design for you or design an alternative.

WEDDING CAKE

The wedding cake is an integral part of the day and this summer cake is designed to tie in with the bridesmaids' arrangements shown earlier—the colors being part of the whole theme.

The design for this two-tier cake (ABOVE RIGHT) consists of white "Bianca" roses with the delicate scent and colorings of blue "Muscari" grape hyacinths entwined with white "Snowflake" wax flowers (*Chamelaucium*), and a hint of the striking "Blue Bee" delphinium. The flowers and foliage have a slight hint of lemon scent. The arrangement is finished

These combine to create a quite beautiful effect. A variety of foliages, including the wispy, wild-looking bear grass (*Xerophyllum tenax*), straight bamboo grass, and the lovely deep-green leaf of the aspidistra plant are entwined with the flowers. The arrangement is placed into a novel "broken-glass" effect vase, which is filled with pale pink tissue paper. This all combines to make a beautifully different "thank you" for that special person.

off with a blue crepe bow to highlight the blue bows on the cake.

The designs are constructed in small shallow dishes which are covered with a waterproof coating and filled with wet floral foam. The top tier generally has the smallest display with the designs getting progressively larger down through the tiers.

THANK YOU

This design shows a departure from the old traditional flat-back bouquet of flowers. It is a hand-tied, contemporary design incorporating a vase and comprising white "Casablanca" lilies and the striking pale pink calla lillies (*Zantedeschia*).

AUTUMN WEDDINGS

BRING THE MELLOW scents and warm glow of the autumnal countryside into your wedding theme with a mixed array of seasonal flowers. Memories of the summer linger in the fragrance of the last few roses and aromatic herbs as the woods and fields are ablaze with the colors of sunset. Use the bright, flame-colored flowers, woodland fruits and berries, and russet leaves to bring the season into your arrangements.

Season of mists and mellow fruitfulness!
Close bosom-friend of the maturing sun;
Conspiring with him how to load and bless
With fruit the vines that round the thatch-eaves run.

From *To Autumn* by John Keats (1795–1821)

AUTUMN

Birthday Flowers in Autumn

VIRGO (AUGUST 23—SEPTEMBER 22)

Colors: Navy blue, dark brown, green, violet

Cornflower (*Centaurea*)

Stock (*Matthiola*)

Phlox

Speedwell (*Veronica*)

SCORPIO (OCTOBER 23—NOVEMBER 21)

Colors: Deep red, maroon, scarlet

Hollyhock (*Althaea*)

Boxwood (*Buxus*)—Cut foliage

Chrysanthemum, red

Lily, red (*Lilium*)

LIBRA (SEPTEMBER 23—OCTOBER 22)

Colors: Pale pink, pale blue, pale green, harmonious
    greens

Gentian (*Gentiana*)

Hydrangea

Lupin (*Lupinus*)

Rose, large-headed (*Rosa*)

MEANINGS OF AUTUMN FLOWERS

ASTER—Flower of September—I share your
    sentiments

BELLADONNA—Pride, silence

DAHLIA—Pomp

GARDENIA—Refined

GLADIOLI—Rememberance

MOCK ORANGE—Counterfeit

PHLOX—Uninamity

PINEAPPLE—You are perfect

CHRYSANTHEMUM, red—I love you,
    remember me

SWEET WILLIAM—Gallantry

BRIDES

MODERN

These contemporary-style bouquets have a certain grace and elegance about them that can be detailed and refined or can express sheer simplicity. They are modern-looking and have become increasingly popular and trendy in the last five years or so. They offer a bride a wonderful alternative to the traditional-style bouquets and natural hand-tieds seen so often today. The designs are very sophisticated and would be more suitable for an elegant fitted dress or suit rather than a traditional bridal gown. This design is ideal if you have a very intricate design on the front of your dress and do not want to cover it with a long, flowing, shower arrangement. The colors and textures of the flowers should harmonize with the designs and materials of your dress.

This particular design (RIGHT) is not constructed on a holder but is an upright, hand-tied design with the chosen foliage being an integral part. It consists of the elegant calla lily (*Zantedeschia* "Mango") which is interspersed with creamy white "Bianca" roses and finished with cool, green scindapsus leaves. Bear grass is included to add some shape to the design and to give the feeling of movement.

The arrangement is then carefully tied with green raffia. The design is placed in a crystal vase filled with slices of lemon and marbles at the base purely for display purposes. This modern bridal bouquet could also be used for presentation, such as a thankyou gift, or placed somewhere where fresh flowers can enhance your special day.

TRADITIONAL

The design (PAGE 51) chosen for the autumn traditional bouquet also has a modern element in its use of gerberas. These flowers—with their large, daisy-like blooms—come in all sorts of vivid colors and have become increasingly popular for weddings where they can make a dramatic impact. They can be used in the bridal bouquet or elsewhere, such as for table centers.

The construction itself is known as a "shower" bouquet or sometimes as a "teardrop." This one is made on a holder which is filled with wet floral foam. The bouqet's contents last a lot longer as they are in water and so continue to get the moisture they need to stay in perfect condition.

The design consists of orange "Weirdo" gerberas, red freesias, and orange "Oberon" chincherinchees (*Ornithogalum dubium*). The flowers are combined with ivy (*Hedera helix*), oval-leaved eucalyptus, and variegated pittosporum, and for added effect, are entwined with contorted willow (*Salix*) to give a rustic look.

NATURAL

This passionate and intense bouquet (LEFT), with its rich shades of roses, golds, reds, and terra cottas, is chosen for the natural design for autumn. With roses—meaning romance—this intricate design is perfect for a romantic wedding day. It is a semi-formal hand-tied posy tightly packed full of "Safari," "Tina," and "Paradiso" rosebuds. These are interspersed with hypericum berries ("Autumn Blaze"), for that typically autumn feel, and the spikeyness of grevilla (dyed orange). The arrangement is tightly tied together with natural raffia, and for the finishing touch, gold twine is woven around the flowers. This is a relatively modern approach but creates a beautiful effect.

BRIDESMAIDS

THIS BRIDESMAID'S DESIGN is chosen to go perfectly with the natual autumn bride's bouquet. (BELOW) It is obviously smaller than the bride's and has slightly less content. It includes the same roses —"Safari," "Tina," and "Paradiso"— combined with the hypericum berries and the orange grevilla, all tied together to create the informal posy look. The golden twine is left out of this design to ensure the bride's bouquet is kept unique.

FAR RIGHT: An informal tied posy of sunflowers, barley oats, and poppy heads—a simple alternative to some of the complicated designs of traditional bouquets that end up looking humdrum.

Sunflowers have become increasingly popular in the last couple of years and provide a vivid and bold choice for a fashion-conscious bride. The colors of the bridesmaids' dresses and the style of the wedding day will decide whether you can carry off this flamboyance, but such a courageous choice will certainly give an unusual look to your day.

GUESTS

THE VERY AMERICAN idea of wearing flowers on the wrist is fast becoming a popular idea elsewhere—particularly school and college proms where everybody wants to wear flowers.

This wrist corsage (BELOW) is often worn for a wedding. The completed design is mounted and sewn (or glued—but sewing is safer) onto a piece of satin ribbon. If you are going to do something like this, remember to take a rough measurement of the wrist in question so that the sizing is correct. This particular design contains the beautifully scented yellow "Texel" freesias combined with the vibrant tone of an orange "Trix" rose. The flowers are entwined with "Long Tom" and kenta palm leaves. Leaves are becoming very popular in modern floral arrangements and can be used abundantly.

Hats, hats, hats!—worn for a wide variety of social and sporting occasions—think of horseraces such as Royal Ascot and the Derby, and of course, weddings. Although generally not as popular as they used to be, hats are still an integral part of a wedding day.

Years ago it was considered very unfashionable to be hatless. With today's fashions hats have become more and more exciting for the younger generation.

For this design (RIGHT) we decided to be conservative and work on a traditional reliable straw hat—something that could have been in a family cupboard for years. It is designed using natural and dried materials. Barley, oats, poppy heads (*Papaver*), and small yellow "Santini" chrysanthemums are incorporated. A natural hessian bow is placed at the back of the hat, to complete the look; it also serves to hide the stems of the materials used.

Buttonholes (ABOVE) are, of course, almost always worn at a wedding and are a most versatile accessory. They can be worn or attached to almost any kind of material. This particular one has been made from one flower. It is a simple but unusual gerbera buttonhole worn by a lady but could equally be worn by a man. The wonderfully wacky "Weirdo" gerbera is teamed up with the deep green foliage of *Ruscus aculeatus*.

N.B. Just a reminder—women should wear their buttonholes as illustrated here. Men's buttonholes should be worn stem side down.

RECEPTION

FOR THIS RECEPTION we have gone down the traditional road. In planning floral designs for a reception, so much depends on the style of room. For example, modern single vases filled with a single stem of a flower would look completely inappropriate for a large, grandiose room with high ceilings, On the other hand, an imposing setting would be just right for tall and elegant arrangements—old-fashioned containers filled with large and bold flowers.

BELOW: A traditionally decorated hotel function room with posy designs and a standard top-table display. This type of display is favored by hotels and conference centers when they are doing an all-in package for a wedding. These traditional arrangements can look as stunning as any if used in the right setting and, being autumn, if the colors blend in with the autumnal trees and seasonal foliage.

The plants used in these round-table displays (LEFT) are a mixture of burgundy and cream, including "White Carmit" spray carnations, clove-colored "Desio" carnations, the delicate "Petronella" alstromeria, the stunning dark "Negrita" tulip, and two shades of chrysanthemum—"Reagan Cream" and "Klondike." The foliage used is leatherleaf (*Arachniodes*), variegated pittosporum (*Populas*), naturally scented eucalyptus, soft *Ruscus hypophyllum* and ivy (*Hedera helix*). This shows how ordinary flowers and abundant foliage complement each other to make a lovely display.

The same flowers are used for the top-table arrangement (BELOW RIGHT) but, instead of being round, the arrangement is an elongated design intended to highlight the length of the top table.

TOP-TABLE DECORATION

To decorate the top table, long, soft ruscus (*Hypophyllum*) is looped and attached to the table cloth with pins. (ABOVE RIGHT) To complement the colors of the flowers, the bows that tied the ruscus at each join were made from burgundy-colored waterproof, florists' ribbons. If your table is particularly long, tie two or more pieces of ruscus together with reel wire (see equipment pages). Decorating the top table like this adds an effective finishing touch, especially when the room is very large or very plain.

CONTEMPORARY DESIGN

For something a little different, a contemporary or modern design can look stunning when used correctly and themed with the rest of the floral decorations. For example, tightly

pack together "Weirdo" gerberas and tie them at the neck and the waist with green raffia. Put them in a steel wire vase full of water, with a small pin holder at the base to hold the stems upright (floral foam could be used in the vase as an alternative to the pin holder). Some green-dyed reindeer moss is used to cover the top of the vase with a single head of gerbera (arranged like a buttonhole) placed in it to give the base of the design some depth. This makes an unusual but beautiful table center.

THANK YOU

A hand-tied design (FAR RIGHT) to say those all important wedding thankyous to a flower and chocolate lover—a mother, a grandmother, or a friend. This design has incorporated chocolates with the flowers. Any type of chocolates can be used, providing they are not too heavy. This design consists of crisp green bupleurum, the lemon-scented white "Snowflake" wax flower (*Chamelaucium*), "Red Ruby" gerberas, "Kees Nelis" tulips, yellow "Frisco" roses, and white aster "Casablanca" september flowers. The flowers are combined with the novel mini-pineapples (*Ananas*) and fresh green fan leaves, and the chocolates are incorporated into the design. To complete this novel bouquet, the entire design is gift-wrapped with orange and yellow crepe paper, and tied with a natural raffia bow. It is aqua-packed to ensure that all the stems are in water, essential when the item is going to be sitting around all day waiting to be taken home!

RIGHT: This original hand-tied design would be the perfect thank-you gift for someone who likes something a bit unusual. The design is created around a square wicker cage with the flowers encased in the center.

Designs such as these are very new to the floristry industry but are becoming increasingly popular. The content of this tied arrangement consists of warm "Leonidas" roses, deep red "Red Lion" freesias and cooling double "Echo Geel" cream lisianthus, combined with "Autumn Blaze" hypericum which contains berry-like heads—great for autumn themes. The foliage consists of Sprenger fern (tree fern) and ivy (*Hedera helix*) which is entwined around the design and the cage itself to create the impression that the ivy is growing in and around the design. As a finishing touch, small raffia bows are tied to some of the flowers and foliage to give it a "rustic" appeal.

WINTER WEDDINGS

PASSIONATE, INTENSE, rich shades of reds and greens are the true mark of winter. Scarlet, ruby reds, and crimsons all sum up this wonderful and sensual season. Fine red wines and the feel of warm, romantic, open fires along with seasonal ivy and holly all help to evoke the feel of this festive season. Winter flowers and foliage are all readily available for you to exploit on your wedding day.

> Lilies, that soon in Autumn slipped their
> gowns of green,
> And vanished into earth,
> And came again, ere Autumn died, to birth,
> Stand full-arrayed, amidst the wavering shower.
>
> From *Winter* by Coventry Patmore (1823–96)

Birthday Flowers
in Winter

SAGITTARIUS (NOVEMBER 22 – DECEMBER 21)

COLORS: Rich purple, dark blue, red, royal blue

Globe thistle (*Echinops*)

Carnation (*Dianthus, Dianthus barbatus*)

Golden rod (*Solidago*)

CAPRICORN (DECEMBER 22 – JANUARY 19)

COLORS: Dark green, grey, black, brown, indigo

Cornflower (*Centaurea cyanus*)

Snowdrop (*Galanthus*)

Ivy (*Hedera helix*) – Cut foliage

Forget-me-not (*Mysotis*)

AQUARIUS (JANUARY 20 – FEBRUARY 18)

COLORS: Electric blue, turquoise

Gardenia

Hydrangea

Orchid

Tulip (*Tulipa*)

MEANINGS OF WINTER FLOWERS

AMARYLLIS – Splendid beauty

ANEMONE – Lovesick

GARDENIA – Refined

HEATHER – Good luck

IVY (cut foliage) – Fidelity

MYRTLE – Simple love

SNAPDRAGON – Intrigue

WAX FLOWER – Amiability

STOCK – Lasting beauty

TULIP – Declaration of hopeless love

BRIDES

TRADITIONAL

RIGHT: This traditional bouquet for winter has been chosen for its shape rather than its content. Holder bouquets are still seen as being a bit contrived, but are arguably more natural than those completely wired from start to finish. These holder designs became increasingly popular in the mid to late 1970s in America and much of Europe

The flowers chosen range from shades of bronze through to reds. The design is based around some stunningly warm, terra cotta roses appropriately named "My Lovely." The way in which the flower has opened looks almost unreal. The rose forms the nucleus of this bouquet with the very modern flower Kangaroo paw (*Anigozanthos*—coincidently meaning "plant with unusual flower") being placed in and around the roses to create an interesting effect. The skimmia (*Japonica rubella*), hypericum berries and ivy leaves are added to instill a real winter feel. Although few items are used in this design, the overall effect is of a bouquet bursting with flowers.

MODERN

This modern hand tied posy (SEE PAGE 66) of stunning, tightly packed, flame-red tulips is absolutley bursting with energy. Even though only one flower is used to create the design— the fringe-edged "Abba" tulip—it manages to look incredibly modern and artistic. It makes a statement about the bride being able to choose something pure and beautiful. To create the plait effect, three stems of bear grass (*Xerophyllum tenax*) are plaited together. For the skirt around the edge of the posy silk-like manta leaves are placed all around. Once tightly tied together a red hessian bow is used

Beautifully fresh and crisp, white ("Bianca") roses are used in the center with the varying foliages supplementing the rest of the design. To encourage the roses to really stand out a skirt of golden heart ivy is placed around them. Various foliage is added to give the design a natural and very elegant look. The foliage used is *Hedera helix* "Ivalace"—wild ivy with berries—*Hedera helix* "Jubilee," wonderfully and delicately scented rosemary, and the regal myrtle. (All the royal brides used to carry myrtle in their bouquets because rumor had it that myrtle was a great aid to fertlility.) The complete design is constructed on a bent-handled floral foam holder.

to finish off. N.B. Tulips have become immensly popular for weddings over the past five years, and although spring is the season mostly associated with them, they are readily available between the months of November and May. Tulips are attracted to the light and curve toward it, so be prepared for this to happen when creating a bouquet. Where the tulips are not tightly packed together they will "move."

NATURAL

If a natural yet modern design is something that you are looking for, then this bouquet will meet your requirements. The look of this natural design (RIGHT) is very modern compared to some of today's more traditional bridal bouquet designs. Although this may be regarded as a simple design, it creates a very striking, chic and elegant effect. This bouquet would be a perfect accompaniment to a stylish, highly tailored dress or evening dress rather than the traditional wedding gown.

BRIDESMAIDS

FLOWER HOOPS are making a come-back for bridesmaids after becoming hugely fashionable in the early 1990s. Today's designs are extremely novel and obviously have a more modern approach than their Victorian counterparts. The hoops can be made from plastic, metal or wood and in varying sizes from approximately eight inches upward.

This design (RIGHT) is based on a twenty-one-inch plastic hoop. Golds are becoming a popular choice for the winter months and this hoop is decorated with gold-embossed hessian ribbon to cover the white plastic base. The design has a very rustic feel about it so the hessian was a natural choice. Natural raffia is tied around the hessian to hold it in place and to stop it slipping. Ivy (*Hedera helix*) is entwined all the way around the hoop to give added interest and to enhance the natural look.

White "Colombe de la paix" calla lilies (*Zantedeschia aethiopica*), traditionally used in church arrangements but becoming increasingly popular for weddings, are used here. These flowers, symbolizing purity, originated from Africa but are now grown in Europe and North America, and can look stunning when correctly arranged. To expound the general

theme the lilies are loosely (yet securely) attached to the hoop with small raffia bows, a gold-embossed hessian bow is tied on at the end and the stems of the flowers are left at their natural length. A raffia hoop is attached at the top of the design to facilitate the carrying for the bridesmaid.

The headdress on this little bridesmaid (BELOW) is designed to go with the hoop design. To keep it very simple and natural some ivy (*Hedera helix*) is entwined around a wired and taped hoop (made to the exact measurement of the bridesmaid's head). All is tied together at the back with natural raffia and finished off with a small gold hessian bow, the same as the one used in the hoop. This perfectly complements the hoop and completes the desired effect.

the design of the ball is so intricate, it would suit a fairly plain dress, not one that was busy.

The design is based around the cream "Pistach" roses—the choice of flowers needs to be quite simple otherwise it will become bottom heavy. The dark green leaf of the ivy alternates and makes a lovely contrast against the creaminess of the roses. Some of the ivy and flowers are lightly dusted with gold paint to blend in with the gold of the

This unusual but beautiful, gold-twigged ball, slightly glittered to make it shimmer, is certainly different. (ABOVE RIGHT) It's a beautiful alternative for that all important flower girl! Bridesmaids, particularly the smaller ones, love to be the center of attention, and carrying something really special like this will certainly give them a feeling of importance. Because

ball to give an unusual added effect. The other flower used in the design is the sweet-smelling, cream "Bossa nova" freesia. To complete the effect, and for ease of carrying, a single "Pistach" rose is attached to the top of the ball with a subtle yellow-gold satin bow to finish the look off.

ABOVE: This hand-tied design of roses uses a completely different approach to the other winter designs. It is constructed by tightly packing a variety of vibrant orange roses together to form a posy-like arrangement. Starting with a central rose (this being the focal area), work outward, forming consecutive rows of roses to make the posy look as round as possible. Once the main shape is established, some croton leaves (*Codiaeum* "Mrs. Iceton") are framed around the outside of the design to create an artificial skirt. To complete the arrangement, an orange raffia bow is attached to the design where all the materials are tied together. This bow serves the dual purpose of concealing the binding point and adding decoration.

GUESTS

CHOOSING THINGS for guests to wear on your special day will always be a difficult task, so it is normally easier to let them to choose something for themselves. The following ideas may give some inspiration.

Traditional buttonholes, as worn by millions of people down the years and at weddings all across the world, as well as being one of the most popular adornments, are also among the easiest to make.

ABOVE:
A traditional corsage design made from a couple of "Bianca" white roses, some myrtle, rosemary, *Hedera helix*, and golden heart ivy leaves. This design combines beautifully with the natural winter wedding bouquet and would be particularly nice if worn by a guest such as the mother of the bride.

ABOVE: A buttonhole for a gentleman. This is a single flower that can be fitted into a lapel of a suit with ease. The buttonhole, flower, and foliage are wired (see technique section) and then constructed. This one consists of a very deep terra cotta rose ("My lovely"), some ivy and some unusual *Anigozanthos rufus*—the Kangaroo Paw flower. Once made, the buttonhole is then pinned and ready for use.

RIGHT: A dramatic black hat accessory. The huge rim of this hat affords a large amount of space on which to base the design. To avoid the hat being damaged in any way, all of the flowers are carefully sewn on. Although a painstaking task, it is by far the best way to display the flowers without damaging the hat material. Because the hat makes such a statement in itself, the flowers chosen are quite flamboyant—lime green revert chrysanthemums and roses. One rose is made up as a buttonhole (using the rose leaves as foliage) and sewn onto the front of the hat.

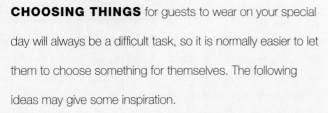

RIGHT: This corsage is for a lady to wear and consists of two roses, hypericum and *Skimmia japonica* "Rubella." The flowers are backed with the leaves from the roses rather than ivy leaves.

RECEPTION

SOME BRIDES DECIDE to make the reception the most stunning part of their day, having the room filled with flowers from top to bottom. At the other extreme, they may decide to have no flowers at all and maybe decorate with just a few balloons. At the end of the day, whatever is decided is really a reflection of the bride's personality.

For the winter months there is a huge variety of flowers and foliage available. There are, however, a few important decisions to be made. If you are getting married in December, do you go for Christmas themes—such as candle arrangements brimming with holly, ivy, and an assortment of berries? Golds always spring to mind at this time of year, with warm reds and voluptuous greens all readily available.

Because these months are obviously cooler than the other seasons of the year, then it is generally a good idea to "warm up" your reception venue. For this reason candles are often chosen as part of the display.

N.B. If candles are chosen, then check with the venue that there are no strange fire risk rules and regulations where candles are concerned.

The winter design chosen here (ABOVE RIGHT) shouts warmth and color. The contrasts of deep reds and cool greens and the use of terra-cotta pots create a warming effect. The depth of the pots allows a nice height and flow to the designs. The main flowers used are the rich "My lovely" terra-cotta roses with the unusual flame-red kangaroo paw (*Anigozanthos rufus*) to complement the color scheme. Red *Alstromeria* "Cobra" is incorporated with pittosporum and soft *Ruscus racemosus* to offset the colors of the flowers. Ivy (*Hedera helix*) plays a major part in the theming of this wedding and is draped all over the edges of the pots. For a little extra some contorted willow (*Salix*) is added to the designs. (Contorted willow is becoming ever more popular and used in every-day designs as well as the more unusual bridal arrangements.) Natural raffia is loosely tied into small bows and attached to some of the flowers.

TOP TABLE DECORATION

The same flowers are used to create the design seen in the top picture on page 72, but using a flat tray instead of a terra-cotta pot. This enables the creation of a much longer

and flatter design for the simple reason that the arrangement should not obscure the bride and groom from their guests.

TOP-TABLE SWAGS

Here long pieces of ivy are used to enhance the top table (BELOW LEFT). The ivy is entwined with long strands of soft ruscus (*Ruscus racemosus*) and carefully attached to the table cloth with natural raffia bows. This decoration reflects the small bows that are attached to the guests' table arrangements.

WEDDING CAKE

Many florists are loth to undertake the time-consuming chore of designing floral arrangements for cakes, but if you are having fresh flowers on your wedding day, then why not have some lovely fresh flowers on your cake?

The obvious way is by using sugar icing that can look as effective as fresh flowers. However, silk flowers, which can look cheap and tacky if not carefully matched with the rest of your flowers, should be treated with caution.

ABOVE RIGHT: For the winter cake, lush deep greens and crisp whites are used to create a fresh, woodland look. The two colors contrast beautifully and complement the color of the icing on the cake. It is best to keep cake designs nice

This stunning hand-tied bouquet consists of the immensely popular "Lynx" gerberas, "Grand gala" red roses, "Jazz" orange roses, the wonderfully delicate and paper like "Fuji deep blue" purple lisianthus, "Royal Fantasy" peach lilies, "Santini" yellow chysanthemum, and "Long Tom" (*Leucandendron*). These are all combined with bear grass (*Xerophyllum tenax*), eucalyptus —both natural and dyed red—seasonal variegated holly, hard *Ruscus hypoglossum* and some natural grevilla. The completed design is topped off with a flame-colored satin bow. This design has not been wrapped in cellophane or other trimmings but left looking natural with the "just made" look.

There is a wide range of floral content available for this type of design and it can be made to look modern, unusual, or downright wacky.

and simple, nothing too intricate, as the cake has its own importance and should not be overshadowed.

This cake only has two tiers and the designs are tailor-made for it. They are made on shallow, waterproof, dishes covered with extra protective coating to ensure that they do not leak (an obvious imperative). Floral foam is put into the dishes and secured.

The design for the top tier consists of white "Tineka' roses, white "Elegance" freesias, pittosporum (*Tobira*), leatherleaf (*Rumohra*), *Ruscus aculeatus*, and oval-leaved eucalyptus. The bottom tier consists of the same materials minus the freesias. The interesting abundance of foliage in these designs adds to the overall effect.

DECORATING A CHURCH

THERE ARE MANY exciting and different ways to decorate a church—the options tend to be limited by the dimensions of the building as well as your budget. It is worth noting that seasonal flowers will work out a lot cheaper than expensive hot-house varieties. Using plenty of varied yet beautiful foliage will also keep the costs down. If your budget is tight, limit your arrangements—perhaps to one in the entrance, the pew ends (it is not necessary to decorate all of them) to create a floral walkway for the bride and her entourage, and either side of the chancel steps or the location of your vows. It might be possible to greet the bridal party and the guests with a pedestal arrangement in the porch or just inside the church door to one side of the aisle, saving other costly arrangements.

The main focus of attention is the altar or chancel steps where the marriage vows are traditionally taken. A pair of pedestal arrangements, either side of the steps, that can be seen by the entire congregation, will create a stunning backdrop to the ceremony. In many old churches there is a natural arch separating the altar, the organist, and the choir from the altar steps. Decorating this arch with a floral display can have the effect of framing the wedding ceremony and creating a beautiful tableau.

ARCHWAY DESIGN

The arch shown here (LEFT) is chosen to look elegant and striking, yet simple. Only three flowers are used to create this magnificent display and is designed on a floral foam garland (small plastic cages all joined safely together). Here the flowers enhance the colors of the dark wood of the church. Creams and foliage are chosen as white would look too stark against the color of the church's wooded beams.

The fragrance of this arch design comes from the sweetly scented "Ophir" freesias—these tiny flowers look perfect against the other flowers chosen. The beauty of the design is created by the delicately bell-shaped "Echo Geel" lisianthus, which despite the delicate and papery look of the heads is surprisingly hardy. Heavily scented dill (often confused with fennel or cow parsley) is added to the arrangement. Dill (*Anethum*) is arguably a "foliage" but is also seen as a flower. (N.B. It is not the norm to use dill with its overpowering scent with another scented flower

but in the large area in which the arch was displayed it was acceptable. It gives the design a certain country garden feel.

The freesias, lisianthus, and dill are supported by the wonderfully versatile ivy (*Hedera*) combined with the luscious green, glossy leaves of the *Ruscus racemosus*. To add variety and enhance the color of the flowers, variegated pittosporum are used.

PEDESTAL DISPLAYS

The choice of flowers displayed in a church on a wedding day is a very individual decision. If you feel the church needs brightening up with large displays of flowers, then pedestal designs are the ideal thing to have (ABOVE). Although sometimes expensive, they are well worth every penny. They are bold, rather special and will dominate at a wedding.

The arrangements here are designed in large dishes and packed with floral foam. (Sometimes the foam is covered with chicken wire for added support.) The flowers used are similar to those used in the archway design (on page 74). Freesias would have got lost in a design this size so are not used. "Pompeii" lilies are used to add scent to the arrangement. These flowers have a beautiful cream star running through the middle of them and complement the other cream flowers—lisianthus and the long, off-white "Teach in" gladioli. White "Reagan" chrysanthemums and spray carnations (*Dianthus* "Medea") are used to fill in the design and make it more cost effective. White wax flower (*Chamaelaucium* "Snowflake") with its beautiful, aromatic lemon-like petals, is the other flower used in the arrangement. The foliage consists of ivy, pittosporum, ruscus, and contorted willow.

PEW ENDS

Think carefully about decorating pew ends—you have to take into account the size and shape of the church. Some have dozens of pews all with potential for decoration (LEFT), while others may have few pew ends, and those impossible to decorate. Decorated pew ends can give the aisle a certain magnificance, almost like little lights guiding the bride to her destiny.

Pew-end cages (see equipment section) are used for these tear drop-shaped designs—the flowers are "Echo geel" lisianthus, "Ophia" freesias, "Eskimo" spray carnations, and "Turban" buttercups (*Ranunculus*) are used with a single cream rose in the center as a focal point. A mixture of ivy, pittosporum, ruscus, and contorted willow is used for foliage.

ALTAR ARRANGEMENTS

LEFT and BELOW: It is not uncommon to have the altar itself decorated. Simple vases of flowers could be used but the design shown here is more formal and uses the same mix of flowers and foliage used in the designs above.

The church plays such an important and integral part in your special day, why not have it decorated from top to bottom with your favorite, sweet-smelling fresh flowers? As an overall picture it looks beautiful and very dramatic, so go for it and make the church literally burst with flowers.

FLOWERS AND PLANTS

FLOWER MEANINGS

Amaryllis—*Splendid beauty*

Anemone—*Lovesick*

Aster—Flower of September—*Virtue*

Bachelor's Buttons, Cornflower—
Celibacy

Belladonna—*Pride, silence*

Calla Lily—*Magnificent beauty*

Carnation—Flower of January

white = *Pure love, truth*

white = *Remember me*

white = *Good luck gift to a
woman*

yellow = *Slighted love*

pink = *Woman's love*

purple = *Capriciousness*

red = *Unrequited love*

striped = *Refusal*

Chrysanthemum—Flower of
November

red = *Remember me, I love you*

white = *Fidelity, truth*

yellow = *I'm sorry*

yellow = *I'm sad*

Columbine—*Folly*

Daffodil—Flower of
March—*Regard,
hope*

Daisy—Flower of April—
Innocence, beauty

Delphinium—Flower of
July—Larkspur—*Appreciation*

Fern—*Sincerity*

Forget-me-not—*True love*

Foxglove—*Insincerity*

Freesia—*Friendship, trust*

Gardenia—*Amiability*

Gardinia—*Refined*

Gladiolus—Flower of August—
Remembrance

Iris—*Promise*

Lavender—*Distrust*

Lily—Flower of July

white = *Purity, virginity*

yellow = *Gratitude, gaiety*

Love-in-the-mist—*Perplexity*

Snapdragon—*Presumption*

Stock—*Lasting beauty*

Sunflower—*Splendid*

Sweet William—*Gallantry*

Tulip—*Fame*

Tulip—Flower of Spring

    red = *Declaration of love*

    yellow = *Hopelessly in love*

    white and red = *Unity*

Violet—Flower of February—*Virtue*

Violet—*Modesty*

Yarrow—*War*

Michaelmas

Daisy—

    Afterthought

Orchid—*Beauty*

Pineapple—*You

are perfect*

Poinsettia—

Christmas Flower (North

America)—Flower of the Holy Night (Mexico)—*Mirth*

Rose—Flower of June

    red = *True love, desire*

    white = *Spiritual, true love*

    black = *Farewell, death*

    yellow = *Friendship*

    pink = *Sweetness*

    thornless = *Love at first

sight*

    single full bloom rose

    = *I love you, and I

still love you*

    variegated rose=

beautiful eyes

Scabious—*Unfortunate love*

Snapdragon—*Intrigue*

FOLIAGE PLANTS

ANTHURIUM

A. andreanum,
A. crystallinium,
A. scherzeranium

SEASON: All year round.

COLOR: Dark green with midribs and veins in ivory above, and pale pink underneath.

LONGEVITY WHEN CUT: 10–18 days.

Tiny heart-shaped ornamental leaves which can be quite difficult to obtain as they are often damaged on the plant.

ASPARAGUS

The many varieties of this plant provide a wide range of small-leaved, needled and feathery ferns.

Smilax, Greenbriar

A. asparagoides, A. asparagoides medeolides.

SEASON: May be limited to spring and summer months.

COLOR: Bright green.

LONGEVITY WHEN CUT: 7–10 days.

Oval leaves smaller and a lighter green than the other Asparagus varieties. Also has a shorter cut life than the other varieties.

Ming Fern

A. densiflorus, A. densiflorus myriocladus.

SEASON: All year round.

COLOR: Green.

LONGEVITY WHEN CUT: 20–28 days.

A branched and heavily tufted foliage. An especially long-lasting variety of Asparagus.

Sprenger Fern, Sprengeri (Tree fern)

A. densiflorus, A. densiflorus sprengeri

SEASON: All year round.

COLOR: Dark green.

LONGEVITY WHEN CUT: 14–20 days.

Needle-like leaves and tiny, sharp thorns are set closely together.

Asparagus Fern, Lacy Fern, Plumosa

A. setaceus, A. setaceus plumosus

SEASON: All year round.

COLOR: Dark and light shades of green.

LONGEVITY WHEN CUT: 14–20 days.

A feathery variety.

ASPIDISTRA Cast iron plant

A. elatior.

SEASON: All year round.

COLOR: Deep green and variegated with cream stripes.

LONGEVITY WHEN CUT: 14–21 days.

Tough and resilient with long leaves that are often washed and treated to give a more shiny appearance.

BUXUS Box, English/ Korean/ Japanese boxwood

B. sempervirens, B. microphylla koreana,
B. microphylla japonica

SEASON: All year round.

COLOR: Glossy dark green. Variegated white and variegated yellow varieties.

LONGEVITY WHEN CUT: 10–14 days.

Small oblong and oval leaves on woody branches.

Oregonia

B. sempervirens

SEASON: All year round but less common in summer.

COLOR: Green variegated with white.

LONGEVITY WHEN CUT: 10–14 days.

Variegated variety of Boxwood.

CODIAEUM Croton

C. variegatum pictum

SEASON: All year round.

COLOR: Multi-colored combinations ranging from pink, red, orange and almost black, to green with white or yellow spots.

LONGEVITY WHEN CUT: 7 days.

Variegated leaves available in various shapes from linear to ovate and in various colors and sizes.

CYCAS Palm, Sago palm

C. revoluta

SEASON: All year round.

COLOR: Dark green.

LONGEVITY WHEN CUT: 21–28 days.

Stiff palm leaves borne on a straight stem. They turn a light, creamy-brown color when dry.

CYPERUS Umbrella grass, Palm crown

C. alternifolius

SEASON: All year round.

COLOR: Green.

LONGEVITY WHEN CUT: 21–28 days.

"Umbrellas" of thin, arching leaf-like bracts at the end of a clump of long, stiff, dark green stems.

CYPERUS PAPYRUS

SEASON: All year round.

COLOR: Green.

LONGEVITY WHEN CUT: 21–28 days

Short, stiff, grass-like inflorescences at the top of tall, thick, dark green stems to form globulous heads.

EUCALYPTUS Gum tree, Silver dollar, Mallee, Eucalyptus

SEASON: All year round, less common in summer.

COLOR: Green, silver-green, blue-green.

LONGEVITY WHEN CUT: 10–14 days.

There are many different varieties of Eucalyptus with a range of leave shapes—oval (*E. populus, E. stuartina*), long (*E. parvifolia, E. nicolli*), round (*E. perrinana*) and double leaved (*E. cinera, E. gunni*).

EUONYMUS (Spindle)

E. japonicus, E. fortuneri

SEASON: All year round.

COLOR: Green, variegated-white—"Silver Queen," variegated-yellow—"Yellow Queen."

LONGEVITY WHEN CUT: 14–21 days.

Leathery, shiny, oval leaves which grow close together on very tough stems.

HEDERA Ivy

H. helix

SEASON: All year round.

COLOR: Foliage—green, variegated-white, variegated-yellow.

FLOWERS: Golden flower turning black. Curly, pointed or heart-shaped leaves.

Ivy looks sensational in shower bouquets and tablecenters. Sometimes sold in bunches, whole plants are more suitable for work in corsages and other bridal work.

ILEX Holly

I. aquifolium

SEASON: November and December.

COLOR: Green, variegated-white, variegated yellow. Bearing red or white berries

LONGEVITY WHEN CUT: 10–16 days

Glossy, dark green leaves with sharp spines.

MYRTUS Myrtle

M. communis

SEASON: All year round. Peak—Winter—early Spring.

COLOR RANGE: Green, variegated variety has white-edged leaves.

Leaves have a pleasant spicy scent when crushed. The variegated variety has smaller leaves.

NEPHROLEPIS Sharon fern

A variety of sword-shaped ferns which vary in shape, length and color.

SEASON: All year round.

COLOR: Green.

LONGEVITY WHEN CUT: 10–14 days

Sword fern, Boston fern

N. exalta "Bostoniensis"

Short, pale green leaves.

Oregon fern, Flat fern, Brake fern, Ladder fern

N. exalta cordifolia

Longer and darker green than the Boston fern. Ferns makes a perfect backdrop to bouquets, table centers or venue arrangements.

PITTOSPORUM Australian laurel, Mock orange, Pitt

P. tobira

SEASON: All year round.

COLOR: Medium-to light green, variegated-white, variegated-yellow/cream.

LONGEVITY WHEN CUT: 10–18 days.

Leathery leaves with very tough stems. Clusters of small yellow flowers bloom in the summer.

RUMOHRA Leather fern

R. adiantiformis

SEASON: All year round.

COLOR: Green.

LONGEVITY WHEN CUT: 14–21 days.

Extremely tough, popular leatherleaf fern also known as African fern or elephant fern. Large, wide fronds, paler and less stiff than the glossy, dark leaves of the American leatherleaf (*Arachniodes adiantiformis*).

RUSCUS Butcher's broom, Box holly

R. aculeatus, R. hypoglossum, R. racemosus

SEASON: All year round, less common in summer.

COLOR: Dark green.

LONGEVITY WHEN CUT: 10–14 days.

Glossy, oval leaves. *R. aculeatus* has smaller, more pointed leaves than *R. hypoglossum*.

Alexandrian laurel, Soft Ruscus

R. racemosus

SEASON: All year round.

COLOR: Dark green. Often producing yellow flowers in early summer and round, orange-red berries in autumn.

LONGEVITY WHEN CUT: 10–14 days.

Long, pointed, dark-green, shiny leaves. As with other species of Ruscus they are not really leaves but flattened shoots.

XEROPHYLLUM Bear grass

X. tenax, X. texanum

SEASON: All year round.

COLOR: Green.

LONGEVITY WHEN CUT: 10–20 days.

Also known as Dasylirion. Very slender, pointed green grass. Creates a stunning effect when hanging decoratively from shower bouquets.

SPRING FLOWERS

ACACIA Mimosa

A. dealbata

AVAILABILITY: Winter and Spring.

COLOR RANGE: Yellow.

FLOWERS: Tiny petal-less flowers in globular clusters with delicate foliage. Typically formed in slender panicles or small round balls.

❖ Acacia is from the pea family and means "prickly tree." Its flowering branches have a sharp, sweet fragrance. Perfect for bouquets and headpieces.

DIANTHUS Carnation

D. caryophyllus

AVAILABILITY: All year round.

COLOR RANGE: Pink, purple, red, white, two-toned. Striated, speckled, or edged.

FLOWERS: Single-flower head per stem or several flowers to a stem (spray carnations).

❖ Dianthus ("divine flower") have been famous for their beauty since classical times. They are amongst the top five of the most cultivated flower and are commonly used as buttonholes at weddings with the smaller spray carnations used to give a splash of color to bouquets.

HYACINTHUS Hyacinth

H. orientalis

AVAILABILITY: Late Autumn to Spring.

COLOR RANGE: Violet, blue, crimson, pink, cream, white.

FLOWERS: Dense spike of tiny, bell-shaped tubular blooms on a single stem.

❖ Named after Huakinthos, the young friend of the god Apollo who was fatally wounded in a discus throwing event. Greek mythology tells of a flower springing up where he fell and Apollo naming it after his young friend. These heavily scented flowers are gaining popularity with late- winter and early-spring brides and create a striking effect in bouquets or tablecenters.

NARCISSUS Daffodil and Jonquil

AVAILABILITY: Autumn to Spring.

COLOR RANGE: Shades of yellow, white, and two color with yellow or white petals and orange, apricot or pink trumpets.

FLOWERS: The family of Narcissi can be divided into eight major groups distinguishable by their flower shape. The simplest way of categorising the type is whether the flower head is single-flowered or double-flowered.

❖ The wild Narcissus was first cultivated by the Romans but now are grow extensively, in many varieties, in the UK, Channel Islands and Holland. They are amongst the top five of the most cultivated flower. The bright yellow daffodil is ideal for decorating the wedding venue while the jonquil (also available in white) works best in arrangements.

PAPAVER Poppy

P. nudicaule

AVAILABILITY: Spring and Summer.

COLOR RANGE: White, pink, apricot, orange, yellow, red.

FLOWERS: Cup-shaped blooms made up of four papery, overlapping petals tapering towards the base.

❖ The commercially cultivated varieties, with their tissue paper textured petals, are smaller than the common red poppy. Grown all over Europe and eastern Asia they have been cultivated since the early eighteenth century. These flowers are guaranteed to give a splash of color to any bridal bouquet.

ROSA Rose
AVAILABILITY: All year round.
COLOR RANGE: Wide variety of colors and shades, practically every color but blue.
FLOWERS: Commercially grown roses can be divided into four main groups; Large-flowered including "Sonia," "Jacaranda" and "Veronica"; Medium-flowered including "Gerdo" and "Europa"; Small-flowered including "Disco" and "Sabrina"; Spray roses including "Evelien."
❖ Roses are among the top five most cultivated and most popular flowers available. Thousands are cultivated every year by commercial growers and hundreds of roses are used to create new varieties. This most romantic flower is a long-standing bridal favorite. Can be used in all aspects of the wedding flowers.

SYRINGA Lilac
S. vulgaris
AVAILABILITY: Autumn to Spring (white), Winter and Spring (mauve / purple).
COLOR RANGE: White, mauve, purple.
FLOWERS: Tiny, star-shaped white or mauve flowers growing in delicate pear-shaped clusters along the branch. Single or double flowers are borne in pyramidal panicles.
❖ The commercially grown lilac has long, leafless, woody stems and the mauve/purple varieties have a sweet fragrance and are ideal for spring brides.

ZINNIA Youth and Old Age
Z. elegans
AVAILABILITY: Spring to early Autumn.
COLOR RANGE: Bright shades of red, orange, yellow, pink, salmon, white, mauve. Virtually every color except blue.
FLOWERS: Round, multi-petaled with a single head on each stem.
❖ Originating in Mexico they are now widely cultivated in the United States. Will add vivid colors to arrangements for the modern bride.

SUMMER FLOWERS

AGAPANTHUS African Lily,
Lily of the Nile

AVAILABILITY: Summer, Autumn, and
  Winter

Violet-blue flower with large, open,
  bell-shaped head. Enhances bouquets
  or table arrangements.

CONVALLARIA Lily-of-the-valley

C. majalis

AVAILABILITY: Limited availability all year
  round. Peak—Spring to early Summer

COLOR RANGE: White,
  occasionally pink.

FLOWERS:
  Small, bell-
  shaped,
  waxy flowers
  borne in
  several
  clusters.

❖ These delicate flowers
  with a memorable perfume are
  often incorporated into bridal
  headdresses and bouquets and are the
  ideal choice for the traditional bridal
  shower.

DELPHINIUM Larkspur

D. consolida

AVAILABILITY: All year round. Peak—
  Summer.

COLOR RANGE: White, pink, blue.

FLOWERS: A spectacular spike of flowers
  closely packed on each stem.

❖ Soft, pastel blooms and are more
  delicate than standard Delphiniums.
  Looks wonderful in formal or informal
  bouquets.

HELIANTHUS
  Sunflower

H. annuus

AVAILABILITY:
  Summer to early
  Autumn.

COLOR RANGE: Yellow.

FLOWERS: Bold, singly
  borne, long-petalled, daisy-like. Some
  sem-double and double forms exist.

❖ The name comes from the Greek *helios*,
  meaning "sun," and *anthos* meaning
  "flower." Ideal for the modern summer
  bride.

IRIS Iris

I. germanica

AVAILABILITY: Limited availability all year.
  Peak—Spring.

COLOR RANGE: Shades of blue and
  purple with yellow stripes, white with
  yellow stripes, yellow with white stripes.

FLOWERS: Elegant fan-shaped flower.
  The grouping of the two sets of petals
  creates the distinctive flower shape.

❖ Meaning "rainbow," Iris was a
  messenger for the Greek gods.
  There are many different varieties
  available some with a noticeable
  scent, others with none. Best used
  in table centers and venue
  decorations.

LATHYRUS Sweet pea

L. odoratus

AVAILABILITY: Spring and Summer.

COLOR RANGE: White, pink, peach,
  cream, cerise, lilac, purple, red.

FLOWERS: Soft-textured, butterfly-shaped
  petals with a delicate frilled, sometimes
  fluted, appearance.

❖ These pretty spring flowers have a
  delicate, oriental appearance and a
  wonderful perfume and are ideal for
  young bridesmaids.

COLOR RANGE:
White, cream,
yellow, pink, green.
FLOWERS: Single
flowers borne on a
spadix at the end of
the stem.

❖ Originating in
Africa they are now
widely grown in
Europe. The white
varieties have long
been used in church
arrangements and
are popular as bridal
flowers—signifying
purity.

POLIANTHES
Tuberose

P. tuberosa

AVAILABILITY: Summer.

COLOR RANGE: Creamy-white
(buds have natural-pink exterior tint).

FLOWERS: Borne on thick, erect
spikes. Petals grow from a funnel-
shaped tube.

❖ The tuberose, with its very heavy, sweet
fragrance, originated in Mexico and has
been cultivated in southern France for
centuries for the perfume industry. Ideal
for bouquets—the florets look dainty
separated and wired into headpieces.

SCILLA Bluebell

S. campanulata

AVAILABILITY: Spring to early Summer.
COLOR RANGE: Blue.

FLOWERS: Small and bell-shaped flowers
clustered on upright spikes.

❖ The cultivated variety has a greater
profusion of florets than the wild bluebell.
Look their best in hand-tied bouquets.

ZANTEDESCHIA Arum lily

Z. aethiopica

AVAILABILITY: All year round. Peak period
for white—Spring. Peak period for
colored—Summer

AUTUMN FLOWERS

ANEMONE Windflower

A. coronaria

AVAILABILITY: Autumn to Spring.

COLOR RANGE: White, pink, purple, deep red, blue. Bi-colored.

FLOWERS: Velvety, cup-shaped petals surrounding a black center.

❖ The most popular contemporary cut anenome "Mona Lisa," available in several colors, has slightly smaller flowers with darker colored centers than other varieties. A white anenome "The Bride" has a Victorian appeal and suits traditional winter weddings bouquets.

ASTER Michaelmas daisy

A. cordifolius, A. ericoides

AVAILABILITY: All year round. Peak—Autumn.

COLOR RANGE: White, pink, orange, purple.

FLOWERS: Daisy-like.

❖ Used as an intermediary or filler flower in traditional bouquets and arrangements.

CHRYSANTHEMUM

C. morifolium,
  C. indicum

AVAILABILITY: All year round.

COLOR RANGE: White, pink, red, bronze, yellow, purple.

FLOWERS: Many different varieties including single blooms and sprays.

❖ The single, daisy-like chrysanthemum has green center and is useful in

wedding bouquets but has the versatility to be used in all wedding arrangements. All varieties have a strong herbal, scent.

DAHLIA

AVAILABILITY: Summer to early Autumn.

COLOR RANGE: White, pink, red, purple, yellow, bronze, orange; also speckled.

FLOWERS: Single-flowered—single row of petals. Double-flowered—double row of petals. Cactus types—flowers sem-double and the florets are pointed.

❖ This huge variety of bright flowers originated in Mexico and has been cultivated in Europe since

the nineteenth century. Best for late summer and autumn weddings.

DIANTHUS Sweet William

D. barbatus

AVAILABILITY: Spring to Autumn.

COLOR RANGE: White, red, pink, two-color.

FLOWERS: Lots of tiny flowers form a delicate head with colorful, variegated petals.

❖ Of the many varieties grown commercially "Scarlet Beauty" (red), "Pink Beauty" (clear pink) and "Crimson" (dark copper-red) are widely available. Ideal for bright autumn bouquets.

GARDENIA Cape Jasmine

G. jasminoides

AVAILABILITY: Limited all year round.
Peak—Summer.

COLOR RANGE: Creamy-white.

FLOWERS: Waxy, double blooms.

❖ Small, evergreen flowering shrub named after the American botanist Dr. Alexander Garden. The flowers are beautiful for use as button holes and corsages and are ideal for formal bridal bouquets and headpieces.

GLADIOLUS Sword lily

AVAILABILITY: Most of the year.
Peak—Summer and Autumn.

COLOR RANGE: White, pink, orange, red, cream, apricot, purple.

FLOWERS: Funnel-shaped and lily-like flowers which hang from tall elegant spikes.

❖ Originating in Africa with a large variety of colors, the smaller gladioli are gaining in popularity with their suitability for use in bouquets and the strongly-scented flowers create a striking effect in venue decorations.

PHLOX Summer phlox

P. arendsii, p. maculata, P. paniculata.

AVAILABILITY: Late Spring to early Autumn.

COLOR RANGE: White, pink, cerise, purple.

FLOWERS: Freely-borne, salver-shaped .

❖ The garden variety has a sweet scent attractive to insects but the commercial flowers have no perfume.

STEPHANOTIS Madagascar Jasmine

S. floribunda

AVAILABILITY: All year round.

COLOR RANGE: White.

FLOWERS: Waxy flowers borne in axillary panticles.

❖ This fragrant, waxy, pure white flower is much in demand for traditional bridal work and corsages.

WINTER FLOWERS

ANTIRRHINUM Snapdragon

A. majus

AVAILABILITY: All year round.

COLOR RANGE: White, red, pink, orange, yellow, lavender.

FLOWERS: Up to fifteen flowers, close together along the stem spike.

LIFE SPAN: Medium.

❖ These striking spikes of fragrant flowers, available in a wide range of glorious colors, will add vivid splashes of color to the modern bride's floral arrangements.

ERICA Heather

AVAILABILITY: Autumn to early Winter (flowering).

COLOR RANGE: White to deep pink, purple.

FLOWERS: Stiff with plumes of florets.

❖ White heather, symbolizing "good-luck," is popular for weddings, especially for button-holes and corsages at a traditional Scottish wedding.

FREESIA

AVAILABILITY: All year round.

COLOR RANGE: White, cream, yellow, orange, red, mauve.

FLOWERS: Branched spikes of approximately six, funnel-shaped blooms.

❖ This tiny delicate flower renowned for its scent is amongst the top five most cultivated flowers. Used to pretty effect when added to other larger flowers in cascading bouquets or wired into headpieces.

HIPPEASTRUM Amaryllis

Hippeastrum

AVAILABILITY: All year round. Peak—early Spring.

COLOR RANGE: Shades ranging from white and pale pink to bright crimson and deep burgundy. Two-color.

FLOWERS: Trumpet flowers at the end of a long, tubular, foliage-free stem.

❖ These resilient, fragrant and dramatic flowers are ideal for a modern winter wedding and look stunning in table arrangements.

MATTHIOLA Stock

M. incana

AVAILABILITY: All year round.

COLOR RANGE: White, cream, pink, cerise, lilac, purple.

FLOWERS: Bold flowers borne on compact spikes.

LIFE SPAN: Long-lasting.

❖ Crumpled petals are a characteristic of this wonderfully strong scented flower. Ideal for brides wanting pastel arrangements.

TULIPA Tulip

AVAILABILITY: Autumn to Spring.

COLOR RANGE: All colors except blue.

FLOWERS: Vast range of tulips divided into four main categories: Single—single row of petals usually rounded. Double—resembling roses they open to reveal several rows of petals. Parrot—often two or three toned. Lily-flowered—pointed petals resembling lilies.

❖ These immensely popular flowers are native to Turkey and Asia Minor and have been cultivated since the sixteenth century. Holland has for many hundreds of years been the main breeder and exporter of new cultivars. Ideal for the modern bride wanting a simple, unstructured bouquet.

PRESERVATION

A BRIDE MAY THINK she will never forget the transient beauty of her wedding bouquet but the flowers are not the only thing that will fade. A skilled professional in flower preservation can create a beautiful three-dimensional picture of a bouquet and make it look as it did on the big day. All flowers can be preserved in this way, roses, lilies, orchids, etc., and the flowers and foliage will appear fresh. The technique involves photographing the bouquet before dismantling it and then reconstructing it after preservation has taken place. After photographing the bouquet the fresh flowers should be removed from the arrangement as soon after the wedding as possible and the drying process begun.

If necessary a bouquet may be placed in a plastic bag and put in the refrigerator for one night. Do not attempt to have flowers dried that have wilted or are crushed. It may be necessary to purchase more flowers to fill out the bouquet.

Ask your florist to reserve any left-over flowers from the wedding for use in the bouquet. Time required for drying flowers varies with their size, texture, and moisture content. However, any flower will dry within three to seven days. Allow seven for large flowers with many petals, such as marigolds, dahlias, or large rosebuds, and three days for smaller flowers—pansies, forget-me-nots, and field daisies. When drying, pack together those flowers requiring less time to dry in one container and those requiring more time in another. Since humidity can be a problem after drying certain flowers, it is best that they are displayed in a clear plastic or glass container. They can also be displayed in a wide range of frames and colors—yew, mahogany, antique pine, antique gold and silver.

AVAILABILITY OF SEASONAL FLOWERS

Flowers Available All Year Round:

AGERATUM (Floss flower)

ALPINIA (Ginger Lily, Pink Ginger, Red Ginger, Shell Ginger, Torch Ginger)

ALSTROMERIA (Peruvian Lily, Ulster Mary)
❖ Dainty, flared flower available in a variety of colors. Ideal fillers for bouquets, headpieces and arrangements.

ANANAS (Dwarf Pineapple, Ornamental Pineapple, Pineapple, Red Pineapple)

ANENOME (Lily-of-the-field, Poppy Anemone, Windflower)
❖ Large, flat flower head grown in a dazzling array of colors. Ideal for wedding bouquets.

ANETHUM (Dill)

ANIGOZANTHOS (Kangaroo's Paw, Monkey Paw)

ANTHURIUM (Flamingo Flower, Hawaiian Heart, Painter's Palette, Tail Flower)
❖ Striking, upright spike of fragrant, waxy petals. Adds dramatic effect to floral arrangements.

ANTIRRHINIUM (Snapdragon)
❖ Striking spikes of fragrant flowers available in a wide range of glorious colors.

ARACHNIS (Scorpi, Spider Orchid)

ARANTHERA (Scorpion Orchid)

ASTER ERICODES (Michaelmas Daisy)

ATRIPLEX (Orach, Red Mountain Spinach)

BANKSIA (Bird's Nest, Bottlebrush)

BOUVARDIA.
❖ Grows in pink, orange or white (scented). Best used as a filler with other flowers in a bouquet.

BUPLEURUM

CALENDULA (Pot Marigold)

CHRYSANTHEMUM (Boston Daisy, Capensis, Feverfew, Florist's Chrysanthemum, Marguerite, Matricaria, Mums, Shasta Daisy)
❖ Bright,showy heads available in a variety of colors and shapes. A versatile flower popular for weddings.

CHAMAELAUCIUM (Wax Flower)
❖ Delicate tiny, pink flower. Its exquisite aroma adds a new dimension when incorporated into your venue decorations.

CIRSIUM (Cnicus, Plumed Thistle)

CYMBIDIUM (Cymbidium Orchid)

DELPHINIUM (Larkspur)
❖ A spectacular spike of flowers which grows in a variety of colors. Looks wonderful in formal or informal bouquets.

DENDROBIUM (Dendrobium Orchid, Pompadour Orchid, Singapore Orchid)
❖ These orchids add impact to cascading bouquets.

DIANTHUS (Border Pink, Carnation, Chinese Pink, Garden Pink, Pinks, Spray Carnation, Sweet William)
❖ Huge flower heads available in a wide range of colors including two-tones. Popular as buttonholes with the smaller spray carnations used to give a splash of color to bouquets.

EUPHORBIA (Spurge)
❖ Evergreen shrub bearing yellowish-green flowers. Useful additions to bouquets and venue arrangements.

FREESIA
❖ Tiny delicate flower renowned for its scent. Used to pretty effect when added to other larger flowers in cascading bouquets or wired into headpieces.

GARDENIA (Cape Jasmine)
❖ Pure white fragrant flower. Ideal for formal bridal bouquets and headpieces.

GERBERA (Barbeton Daisy, Transvaal Daisy)
❖ Large daisy-like blooms available in a variety of vivid colors. These trendy flowers have become popular and make a dramatic impact in

bouquets or table arrangements.

GLADIOLUS (Gladioli, Sword Lily)
❖ Strongly-scented flowers which hang from tall elegant spikes. Creates a striking effect in venue decorations.

GYPSOPHILA (Baby's Breath, Chalk Plant, Gyp, Maiden's Breath)
❖ An abundance of tiny flowers perfect for all aspects of floral decoration for the wedding.

HELICONIA (Firebird, Lobster Claw, Parrot Flower, Wild Plantain)

HIPPEASTRUM (Amaryllis, Belladonna Lily)
❖ Huge open lily available in shades ranging from white and pale pink to bright crimson and deep burgundy. Fragrant flower which looks stunning in a table arrangement.

IRIS
❖ Elegant fan-shaped flower most commonly blue but available in white and yellow. Best used in tablecenters and venue decorations.

LEUCADENDRON (Flame Tip, Safari Sunset, Silver Tree)

LEUCOSPERMUM (Nodding Pincushion, Pincushion Protea, Sunburst Protea)

LIATRIS (Blazing Star, Button Snakeroot, Gay Feather, Kansas Feather, Kansas Godfather)

LILIUM (Asian Hybrid Lily, Bermuda Lily, Easter Lily, Madonna Lily, Mid-century Hybrid Lily, Oriental Hybrid Lily, Speciosum Lily, Tiger Lily, Trumpet Lily)
❖ Highly fragrant, trumpet-shaped flower which grows in an abundance of glorious colors. This popular wedding flower looks wonderful in bouquets, table arrangements and venue decorations.

LIMONIUM (German Statice, Rat's Tail Statice, Russian Statice, Sea Lavender, Statice)

MATTHIOLA (Gillyflower, Stock)
❖ Available in a range of delicate colors—pink, lavender, lemon and white. Ideal for brides wanting pastel arrangements.

MOLUCCELLA (Bells of Ireland, Shell Flower)

NERINE (Guernsey Lily, Spider Lily)
❖ Open sprays of trumpet-shaped flowers in exotic pinks. These flowers look stunning in tropical bouquets.

ONCIDIUM (Golden Shower Orchid)

ORNITHOGALUM (Chincherinchee, Wind Lily, Star of Bethlehem)

PAPHIOPEDILUM (Cypripedium, Lady's Slipper Orchid, Amabilis Orchid, Cypripedium Orchid, Slipper Orchid)

PHALAENOPSIS (Amabilis, Moth Orchid)

PROTEA (Giant Honey Pot, Giant Wooly Beard, King Protea, Pink Mink, Queen Protea, Sugar Bush)

ROSA (Rose)
❖ This romantic flower is a long-standing bridal favorite.

SOLIDASTER

STEPHANOTIS (Madagascar Jasmine)
❖ Pure white flower with a heady perfume. Used in bouquets and corsages.

STRELITZIA (Bird of Paradise Flower)

ZANTEDESCHIA (Arum Lily, Calla Lily)

LATHYRUS (Everlasting Pea, Sweet Pea)
❖ Available in a whole range of delicate shades. Pretty spring flower is ideal for young bridesmaids.

Flowers Available in Summer, Autumn & Winter:

AGAPANTHUS (African Lily, Lily of the Nile)
❖ Violet-blue flower with large, open, bell-shaped head. Enhances bouquets or table arrangements.

Flowers Available in Autumn, Winter & Spring:

ACACIA (Mimosa, Wattle)
❖ Tiny bunches of yellow balls with delicate foliage. Perfect for bouquets and headpieces.

TULIPA (Tulip)
❖ Available in a multitude of varieties and colors. Ideal for the modern bride wanting a simple unstructured bouquet.

Flowers Available in Spring & Summer:

ALCHEMILLA MOLLIS (Lady's Mantle)
❖ Tiny bright greenish-yellow flowers and pale green leaves with crinkled edges.

CAMPANULA (Bellflower, Canterbury Bell, Chimney Bellflower, Clustered Bellflower, Cup and Saucer Flower, Harebell, Peach-leaved Campanula)

CENTAUREA (Bachelor's Button, Bluebottle, Cornflower, Large-headed Centaurea)
❖ A pretty blue flower ideal for summer bouquets.

DIANTHUS BARBATUS
DORONICUM (Leopard's Bane)

EREMURUS (Desert Candle, Foxtail Lily)
ERIGERON (Fleabane)
GODETIA (Clarkia, Farewell to Spring, Satin Flower)

IXIA (African Corn Lily, Flame of the Forest)

SCILLA (Bluebell, Cuban Lily, English Bluebell, Squill, Wood Hyacinth)
❖ Tiny blue or white bell-shaped flowers. Look their best in hand-tied bouquets.

TRITELEIA (Brodiaea)
❖ Single, slender stem from which lots of delicate flowers emerge. Ideal for dainty, pretty bouquets.

VIBURNUM (Guelder Rose, Snowball Tree)

Flowers Available in Spring, Summer & Autumn:

ALLIUM (Flowering Onion, Garlic, Giant Onion, Ornamental Onion flower)
❖ Flower head is a mass of tiny blossoms which form a huge spherical bloom. Creates a dramatic effect.

AQUILEGIA (Columbine, Granny's Bonnet)

CRASPEDIA (Drumstick)

EUSTOMA (Lisianthus, Prairie Gentian)
❖ Delicate bell-shaped flowers available in every shade from white to purple. Perfect for modern brides wanting a colorful bouquet.

GLORIOSA (Gloriosa Lily, Glory Lily)

HELIANTHUS (Sunflower)
❖ Striking, colorful flower. Ideal for the modern summer bride.

Flowers Available in Summer & Autumn:

ACHILLEA (Common Yarrow, Milfoil, Sneezewort, Yarrow)

ACONITUM (Monkshood)

AMARANTHUS (Cat's Tail, Love-lies-bleeding, Prince's Feather, Tassel Flower)

CALLISTEPHUS (China Aster)

CELOSIA (Chinese Wool Flower, Cockscomb, Prince of Wales' Feather)

COREOPSIS (Calliopsis, Tickseed)

COSMOS

DAHLIA
❖ Bright and showy flower grown in an abundance of colors. Best for late summer and autumn weddings.

ECHINOPS (Globe Thistle)
❖ An enthralling globe-shaped flower head ranging from an unusual metallic shade to bright blue. Ideal for the more adventurous bride.

GOMPHRENA (Globe Amaranth)

HELICHRYSUM (Everlasting Flower, Straw Flower)

HYDRANGEA (Common Hydrangea, French Hortensia)
❖ Large, domed flower heads of four-petal blooms available in white, green, pink, mauve and blue.

HYPERICUM (St. John's Wort)

KNIPHOFIA (Torch Lily, Poker Plant, Red-hot Poker)

LAVANDULA (Lavender)
❖ Dense spikes of fragrant, pale purple, tubular flowers.

LAVATERA (Mallow)

PHLOX (Summer Phlox)

PHYSOSTEGIA (False Dragonhead, Obedient Plant)

RUDBECKIA (Black-eyed Susan, Coneflower, Gloriosa Daisy)

SAPONARIA (Outdoor Gypsophila, Soapwort)

SCABIOSA Drumstick, Pincushion Flower, Scabious, Sweet Scabious)

SEDUM (Stonecrop)
❖ Clusters of tiny star-shaped flowers in shades of yellow, ruby and pink. The leaves with hints of varying hues will add interest to any bouquet, tablecenter or venue decoration.

SOLIDAGO (Golden Rod)

VALOTTA (Scarborough Lily)

ZINNIA (Youth and Old Age)

Flowers Available in Autumn & Winter:

CHRYSANTHEMUM

PARTHENIUM

EUPHORBIA FULGENS (Snow-on-the-mountain)

Flowers Available in Winter & Spring:

AMM (Lace Flower, Queen Anne's Lace)

CHAMAELAUCIUM (Geralton Wax Plant, Tea-tree, Wax Flower)

HELLEBORUS (Christmas Rose, Hellebore, Lenten Rose)

HYACINTHUS (Common Hyacinth, Dutch Hyacinth, Hyacinth)
❖ Dense spike of tiny bell-shaped blooms on a single stem available in soft creams, pinks and blues. Creates a striking effect in bouquets or table-centers.

MUSCARI (Grape Hyacinth)
❖ Small, bright blue clusters of flowers. Ideal for bouquets.

NARCISSUS (Daffodil, Jonquil)
❖ Bright yellow flower abundant during spring—ideal for decorating the wedding venue.

PRUNUS (Flowering Almond, Flowering Cherry, Flowering Peach, Ornamental Plum)

SYRINGA (Lilac)
❖ Tiny, star-shaped white or mauve flowers growing in delicate pear-shaped clusters along the branch. Ideal for spring brides.

Flowers Available in Spring:

CONVALLARIA (Lily of the Valley)
❖ Tiny, bell-shaped flower with a heady fragrance. Ideal choice for the traditional bridal shower.

GENISTA (Broom, Canary Island Broom, Cytisus, Florist's Genista, Warminster Broom)

MAGNOLIA (Magnolia)
  ❖ Pretty blooms available in a huge array of colors and shapes. They can be incorporated with stunning effect to bouquets, headpieces and venue decorations.

RANUNCULUS (Buttercup, French Buttercup, Persian Ranunculus, Turban Buttercup)

VIOLA (Sweet Violet, Violet)
  ❖ Tiny, flat-fronted flower available in shades of deep violet and purple. They look stunning when wired and incorporated into a headpiece or bouquet.

Flowers Available in Summer:

ALTHAEA (Hollyhock, Rose Mallow)
ASCLEPIAS (Blood Flower, Butterfly Weed, Milkweed, Swallow Wort)
ASTIBE
ASTRANTIA (Masterwort)

CARTHAMUS (Safflower)
CHRYSANTHEMUM FRUTESCENS
CROCOSMIA (Montbretia)

DELPHINIUM CONSOLIDA
DIGITALIS (Foxglove)
  ❖ Dramatic 3ft-tall stem topped with an abundance of small pinky, lilac flower heads. Creates a stunning effect when used as a venue decoration.
DIMORPOTHECA (African Daisy, Cape Marigold, Star of the Veldt)

ERYNGIUM (Alpine Thistle, Sea Holly)
EUCHARIS (Amazon Lily, Eucharis Lily)

GENTIANA (Gentian)

HELENIUM (Sneezeweed)

LUPINUS (Lupin)
  ❖ Attractive spikes of yellow flowers. A dramatic choice for adventurous summer brides.
LYSIMACHIA (Loose Strife)

MYOSOTIS (Forget-me-not)
  ❖ Delicate, small blue flowers. Ideal for table arrangements and venue decoration.
NIGELLA (Devil-in-the-bush, Love-in-the-mist)

  ❖ Attractive sky-blue flower surrounded by bright-green foliage. Ideal for brides seeking something different.

PAEONIA (Peony)
  ❖ Beautiful, big red flowers. For the modern bride, a few look spectacular in a hand-tied bouquet.
PAPAVER (California Poppy)
  ❖ Dainty cup-shaped flowers on slender stems available in a variety of colors.
POLIANTHES TUBEROSA (Tuberose)
  ❖ Fragrant, creamy-white flower. Ideal for bouquets; the florets look dainty, separated and wired into headpieces.

SANDERSONIA

TRACHELIUM (Blue Throatwort)

VERONICA (Leptandra, Speedwell)

Flowers Available in Autumn:

ASTER NOVI-BELGII (September Flower)
  ❖ Daisy-like pink or lilac flower usually with a bright yellow center. Adds vibrant color to a wedding bouquet.